This edition is lovingly dedicated by

Asher David Milstein

In memory of his grandparents

Rabbi Elazar Kahanow Z"L ~ Henrietta Milstein A"H

His brother

Betzalel Milstein Z"L

His great uncles

Aaron Kahan Z"L ~ Yankel Basch Z"L

And his great Aunt

Hanka Kozlovsky A"H

And in honor of his parents

Lazer and Ziporah Milstein

His grandparents

Monroe and Judy Milstein ~ Rebbetzin Rochel Kahanow

His brother

Elisha Shlomo Milstein

In Honor of our Dear Parents

Mr. and Mrs. Yehudah Munk

Rabbi and Mrs. Eliyahu Shuman

Who are our role models and source of inspiration

Ezriel and Yaffa Munk

In Honor of our Dear Parents

Jerome and Ruth Kamerman

In Memory of our Dear Parents

Eli and Elaine Soniker Z"L

Mahla and Hilton Soniker and Family

In Loving Memory of

HaRav Tzvi ben R' Pesach Diskind Z"L

Reb Moshe Gershon ben Akiva Yosef HaKohen Eisenberg Z"L

Reb Tzvi Dov ben Yerachmiel Hyman Z"L

Sara bas Levi Hyman A"H

ABOUT THE SORALA FOUNDATION

The Sorala Foundation was created to focus on three aspects of sorely needed financial aid in the Jewish community. The foundation distributes bonuses before Yom Tov to our dedicated teachers who educate our precious children. It provides interest-free loans to those experiencing monetary hardship and grants financial assistance to couples in need of *Sholom Bayis* counseling. To learn more about the foundation please email *emunk@torablinks.org*.

SEEK
PEACE
AND PURSUE IT

SEEK
PEACE
AND PURSUE IT

Proven Strategies to Resolve
Conflicts and Improve Relationships

DOVID LIEBERMAN, PH.D.

VITER PRESS

Published by Viter Press
1072 Madison Avenue, Lakewood, NJ 08701
Email: DavidJay@aol.com Fax: 772-619-7828

ISBN 10: 0-9786313-1-5
ISBN 13: 978-0-9786313-1-4
Library of Congress Control Number: 2009928811

Cover Design & Interior Design: DesignForBooks.com

דוד קאהן

ביהמ"ד גבול יעבץ
ברוקלין, נוא יארק

ב"ה

I have read many chapters of Dr. Lieberman's "Seek Peace and Pursue It". To my mind, an appropriate sub title would be "How to Live".

Rav Yisroel Salanter zt"l, the father of the Mussar movement, maintained that one should fulfill two distinct areas of mussar learning: one for weltanschauung (hashkofo) and one for self awakening (hisorarus). Both scholar and layman will find that this well written book can serve both needs. It is replete with in depth analysis of human behavior (which one can refer to as "kochos hanefesh") which helps the reader gain a proper outlook for his/her purpose in life, and it concommitantly awakens a person not to fall into those spiritual pitfalls that non thinking people are prone to slide into.

My heartfelt blessings to Dr. Lieberman for the success of this masterful book.

בב"ט
פ"ה, יום ג' אל
דוד

Contents

Introduction   ix

A Note to Readers   xi

PART 1
Conversations and Confrontations

1 The Psychology of Conflict   3

2 Overcoming Personality Conflicts   19

3 Reject Advice Without Rejecting the Person   35

4 In Business, Turn a Complaint into a Plus   39

5 When There's Nothing Nice to Say   47

6 How to Offer Constructive Criticism   51

7 How to Handle Unfair Criticism   63

8 Dealing with Emotionally Unstable Individuals   69

9 Communicating Complex Ideas   75

10 Help Someone Open Up and Be More Expressive   79

11 The Gentlest Way to Break Unpleasant News   85

PART 2

Conflict Resolution

12 No More Tug-of-War: When You Both Want
        What's Best   95

13 Simple Methods for Fair and Equitable Division   101

14 The Family Feud over Money: End It Now   105

PART 3

Paving a Path to Forgiveness

15 What to Do When You Say the Wrong Thing   115

16 How to Reestablish Meaningful Relationships   119

PART 4

You Can Be the Great Peacemaker

17 Help Anyone Gain Forgiveness: Strategies for
        Getting One Person to Simply Listen to the Other   135

18 Help to Settle a Deadlock in a Mediation,
        Arbitration, or Negotiation   149

19 Bring People Closer Together, Who Have Either
        Grown Apart or Who Just Don't Get Along   157

20 The Rift: When They Drifted Apart Over
Something Minor or Now Irrelevant 163

21 When Nothing Seems to Work: Six Tactics for
Dealing with the Most Challenging of People
and Situations 171

PART **5**

Harmony at Home

22 The Key to *Shalom Bayis* (Family Harmony) 179

23 Five Foundations of a Successful Marriage 185

24 Raising Happy, Healthy, and Emotionally
Resilient Children 193

25 The Adult Child: Help Your Older Child Eliminate
Self-Destructive Habits 201

26 Techniques to Maximize the Parent and Adult-Child
Relationship 213

FAQs 221

Afterword 225

Glossary 229

Acknowledgements 237

About the Author 239

Introduction

The *Midrash* reveals that *shalom* (peace) is different from other *mitzvos*.[1] Many of the *mitzvos* (Torah commandments) require a certain time and place for their performance. The mitzvah of, "Seek peace and pursue it,"[2] however, is not bound by time. We have to continually strive to promote and maintain peace in our own lives and in the lives of others.

Drawing wisdom from Torah and psychology, *Seek Peace and Pursue It* reveals insights into human nature, and offers a practical system to reduce friction and enhance the most challenging of relationships.

Make a difference today, in your life and in the lives of your neighbors, friends, and loved ones, and as Hillel advises, "Be among the disciples of Aharon, loving peace and pursuing peace, loving people and bringing them closer to the Torah."[3]

---

1. *Devarim Rabbah* 5:15.
2. *Tehillim* 34:15.
3. *Pirkei Avos* 1:12.

A Note to Readers

Two types of strategies are presented in this book: Honest and open techniques that encourage the strengthening of a relationship can and should be used liberally. There are certain occasions, however, as described within these pages, where minor deception or exaggeration are necessary in order to heal rifts and save a person's feelings.

The Torah allows one to distort the truth in order to make or maintain peace.[1] In such a situation, one should make sure that the techniques adopted are used cautiously, and conform to the dictates of *halachah* (Torah law). If you are unsure as to the correct way to proceed, a Rav (a Rabbi qualified to issue halachic rulings) should be consulted.

Rabbi Eliyahu Dessler writes, "There are a number of techniques that people utilize (to get along well with other people). Some of them might seem to be accompanied by ulterior motives, but it is still worthwhile to utilize every possible tool in order to effect a positive transformation of your character traits. As long as your intentions are for the sake of Heaven, in

---

1. Not only is it permissible to alter the truth in the interest of peace, but it is often obligatory (*Yevamos* 65b). Deception cannot be used indiscriminately, however. In the upcoming chapters, we will touch on several cases where bending the truth is permissible.

order to do the will of the Creator, there is no doubt that you
will be helped to eventually gain positive motivations."[2]

⌇

Given the almost endless multitude of variables, not all of the
suggested strategies within these pages are going to be feasible
for every encounter and for every individual. In order to make
this book as accessible and practical as possible, a wide spectrum of approaches is provided, so that in any given situation,
you will be able to apply at least one or two of the techniques
described.

You will find, too, that tactics given in other sections will
also be effective in your specific circumstance. So to round out
your overall strategy look at other chapters that may relate to
your situation.

---

2.   *Michtav m'Eliyahu*, vol. 4, p. 244.

PART **1**

Conversations and Confrontations

The Psychology
of Conflict

W hat do we mean when we say that we are hurt? Or that someone has offended or embarrassed us? What are we trying to express when we say that someone was rude or disrespectful, or did something that was unforgivable?

In simple terms, we are stating that someone else's behavior has caused us emotional pain. But why are we upset by these situations, to begin with? How can the actions of another person—perhaps someone we may not even know, or may not ever see again, or someone we do not even like or respect—cause us to experience such grief?

You don't bleed. It doesn't cost you anything, and you're not prevented from living your life. Yet it matters, and sometimes it matters a lot.

Why Do We Care?

In order to be happy, have good relationships, and be emotionally balanced, a person has to feel good about himself. This means that we need to literally love ourselves. This self-love is called self-esteem.

Self-esteem is a by-product of how you live your life. It cannot be gained directly. It can be gained only through self-respect. Why is this so? If you do not respect yourself, then you cannot possibly love yourself.

How Does a Person Gain Self-Respect[1]

Three inner forces exist within human beings, and they are often at odds with each other: the body, the ego, and the soul.

Doing what is easy or comfortable is a body drive. Examples of overindulgences of this force are overeating or oversleeping—in effect, doing or not doing something we know we should or should not do, merely because of how it feels.

An ego drive can run the gamut from making a joke at someone else's expense to buying a flashy car that is beyond our means. When we are motivated by ego, we do things that we believe project the right image of ourselves. These choices are not based on what *is* good, but on what makes us *look* good.

If we cannot control ourselves and we succumb to immediate gratification or strive to keep up an image, afterwards we become angry with ourselves, and feel empty inside. These emotions erode our self-esteem and corrupt our self-respect.[2]

---

1. The following explanation is excerpted from the author's book, *Real Power* (Viter Press, 2008) pp. 9–11.

2. The body wants to do what feels good; the ego (*yetzer hara* or evil inclination) wants to do what looks good; and the soul (*yetzer hatov* or good inclination) wants to do what is good. Free will is a product of the ensuing conflict between these forces.

    This does not mean we should ignore our body's basic needs. Nourishing one's body and enjoying physical pleasure are in keeping with Judaism. The Talmud (*Yerushalmi Kiddushin* 4:12) states, "R' Chezkiah and R' Kohen said in the name of Rav: in the future (after death) a person will give an accounting for everything which he saw but did not eat." R' Dessler (*Michtav m'Eliyahu*, vol. 3, p. 153) explains: we will be called to account for renouncing any permissible

To compensate for these feelings of guilt and inadequacy, the ego engages and we become egocentric. As a result, our perspective narrows, and we see more of the self and less of the world; this makes us increasingly more sensitive and unstable.

We only gain self-esteem when we are able to make responsible choices, and do what is right, regardless of what we feel like doing or how it appears to others—this is a soul choice. In turn, we rise to a higher and healthier perspective, because self-esteem and the ego are inversely related; like a see-saw, when one goes up the other goes down.[3]

How It All Fits Together

Herein lies the basis for every type of interpersonal conflict. Because human beings are, in fact, wired to like themselves, when we cannot nourish ourselves—by making good choices and gaining self-respect—we turn to the rest of the world to "feed" us.

---

pleasure that would have helped us appreciate our Creator and improve our service of Him.

On the other hand, abuse or overindulgence is not healthy and leads to the deterioration of our wellbeing, as the Gemara teaches: "Alexander asked the Elders of the South what a man should do to live. They replied, 'Let him deprive himself (being righteous).' He asked what a man should do to deprive himself. They replied, 'Let him live (in self-indulgence)!'" (*Tamid* 32a). It is necessary, therefore, to maintain a balance and satisfy one's physical needs in moderation.

3.   Difficult times and tragic events challenge our coping skills. As humans, our perspective is finite; therefore, complete understanding is elusive. Still, we can gain peace of mind and comfort even in difficult times by considering that everything is connected and purposeful. Imagine the wings of a butterfly magnified a thousand times. Looking at it from close up, we can't tell what it is, what it does, or why it exists. We must move back to see what it really is. Then, its design, the details, and purpose become clear. The wings are part of a larger organism. Everything begins to make sense when we utilize our gift of perspective. A healthier self-esteem accelerates the process, naturally widening our perspective because of its inverse relationship to the ego—which blocks perspective.

This nourishment that we need comes in the package of respect. We desperately, but erroneously, believe that if other people respect us, then we can respect ourselves. Self-esteem and ego both pivot on respect. We need it from somewhere, and if we don't get it from ourselves we demand it from others.

The great *Mussar*[4] leader, Rabbi Simchah Zissel Ziv, writes, "If you observe people carefully you will see that someone who loves the approval of others will, as it were, sell himself as a slave to those who flatter him. He will not even realize what is happening to him, however obvious it may be to an outside observer."[5]

The less a person likes himself, the more dependent he is upon the rest of the world to make him feel good. This is why a person with low self-esteem is highly sensitive—because his opinion of himself fluctuates with his ability to impress others. When we are at the mercy of others for proof of our worth, we become tense and vulnerable, as we interpret and over-analyze every fleeting glance and casual comment.

When you enjoy higher self-esteem, you are not as quick to take umbrage,[6] or you realize that maybe the person who caused offense has his own hang-ups and issues. Simply stated, if you have higher self-esteem (a) you don't assume that his actions mean he doesn't respect you, and (b) even if you do come to

---

4.   *Mussar* is the practice of personality development (through exercising moral discipline) within the Jewish tradition, the end goal being perfection of character, cultivation of morality, and emulation of Divine qualities.

5.   Rabbi Simchah Zissel Ziv Broida, *Chochmah u'Mussar*, vol. 1, p. 219.

6.   In his book, *Prisoners of Hate*, Aaron Beck writes, "Depressed patients often relate irrelevant events as a sign of their own unworthiness or imperfections." His findings reinforce the idea that those who suffer from low self-esteem and depression have a warped perspective and understanding of their world and those who occupy it. See A. T. Beck, *Prisoners of Hate: The Cognitive Basis of Anger, Hostility, and Violence* (NY: Harper Collins, 1999), p. 28.

Public Speaking

Public speaking is ranked as the number-one fear—even above death. Since the speaker is not in control of how the audience perceives him, he doesn't know what they are thinking about him, and this makes him uneasy. For this reason, we can speak more easily one-on-one because we are able to see instantly the person's reaction and so we feel more in control of the situation. But as the size of the audience increases, the ability to accurately gauge the audiences' perception decreases. Feedback gives us direction and a greater sense of control.

that conclusion, you aren't angered, because you don't *need* his respect in order to respect yourself.[7]

Why Is Anger the Emotional Response?

When a person gets angry, it is because he is, to some extent, fearful. And this fear comes from the fact that he has lost control of some aspect of his life—of his circumstance, his understanding of his world, or his self-image. The response to fear—the ego's attempt to compensate for the loss—is anger.

---

7. It is fundamental to our emotional and spiritual wellbeing to maintain the healthiest possible relationships with our immediate family—parents, siblings, spouse, and children. While all relationships are important, familial relationships are crucial; strive to make them as positive and healthy as possible. Even with high self-esteem, we desire the love and respect of those who know us best. We unconsciously wonder, *If this person treats me like this, and he knows the real me, then what am I worth?* Therefore, those who are closest to us rely on us most, and need the love and respect of those who know them best.

All conflicts, whether in personal or professional relationships, arise from the following sequence of events:

First there is the **event** or **catalyst** that results in an
undesirable and unexpected outcome; this produces a
loss of control, which make us anxious and **fearful**.
The lower our self-esteem, the more fearful we
become. As a result of our fear, we become **angry**. This
destructive emotion often serves as a mask for other
negative emotions, such as jealousy and guilt, and can be
directed inwardly at oneself or outwardly.[8]

Let's look at a diverse set of circumstances that can lead to conflict and see how the process unfolds in a consistently similar
way.

Real-Life Scenarios

▪ **Your employee steals** (catalyst). ➡ This was obviously
not on your agenda, as it clashes with how you expect a

---

8.   In general there are four ways a person can choose to respond to conflict:
(1) accept (2) retreat (3) surrender, or (4) fight. The first possible response is the
healthiest one: accept. He understands the situation and responds appropriately
and responsibly; he does not become angered and emotional. A passive-
aggressive person is generally described as one who would retreat to avoid the
confrontation. He is unable to face the situation head-on, so he chooses to back
down, only to get back at the person in another way, at another time—whether
it is by being late, "forgetting" to do something important for the person, or
just generally inconveniencing him. A third possible response is surrender.
This is where he simply gives up and gives in. This response often produces
codependency and a doormat mentality in the relationship. He doesn't feel
worthy to stand up for himself and/or feels that he is unable to advance his
own agenda, needs, and wishes. And last, the fourth is fight. Here we have the
response that produces direct and unhealthy conflict. This person chooses to
battle it out, emotionally charged and enraged.

worker to behave, and you lose control of the situation. ➡ This causes you to become fearful of what happened to you, or what might happen to you and to the relationship. ➡ Consequently, you are angered.

■ **Someone cuts you off on the road** (catalyst). ➡ You lose control of the situation, as you had to swerve or hit your brakes in order to avoid an accident. ➡ This causes you to become scared, thinking of "what might have happened." ➡ The result is then anger directed at the other driver.

■ **Your child refuses to wear her warm jacket** (catalyst). ➡ You feel that you are not in control of the situation. ➡ You may become fearful that she does not respect you and will not listen to other things that you ask her to do. ➡ You then become angry with her for not listening to you.

■ **A person is rude to you** (catalyst). ➡ Depending on who it is, this act of disrespect may cause you to doubt yourself. ➡ To some extent, you may become fearful that he doesn't like or respect you, and this causes you to question your own self-worth and image. ➡ You become angered because the way you wish for others to treat and relate to you is different from how the situation is evolving.

Our need to feel in control also extends to situations that have nothing to do with other people. For instance:

■ **You trip over a chair in the dark** (catalyst). ➡ You lose control—meaning that your plan to walk from point A to point B without tripping was disrupted. ➡ This caused you to become scared, as you may have injured yourself. ➡ You then become angry. (Interestingly, some people become angry at themselves, at the chair—kicking it—or even at the person who put it there for you to trip over.)

Logically, anger offers no real satisfaction or psychological comfort. It is our ego's defense mechanism to feeling vulnerable, yet we spiral out of control, and become weaker with each intense, anger-driven thought or action.[9]

On the Spiritual Side

We have already seen from a psychological perspective how an abdication of self-control impacts on our emotional solvency and the quality of our relationships. The spiritual impact is no less potent.

Feeling a loss of control creates an upheaval for our psyche as well as our soul. Why is this so? The more we resemble our Creator, by emulating His ways, the closer we move towards God. This is because closeness is not measured in terms of physical space, but rather through levels of awareness that manifest through similarities.[10]

God, being non-physical, does not have a form, so what do we mean when we speak of man being created in the image of God?[11] It means that human beings have the freedom to forge their own reality. In that way we resemble God, Who is

---

9. "A man's intellect makes him slow to anger" (*Mishlei* 19:11); "If you do not get angry, you will not sin" (*Berachos* 29b).

10. Cf. Rabbi Moshe Chaim Luzzato, *Derech Hashem* 1:2:2.

11. Fostering awareness of our own greatness is not an optional undertaking. Our Sages teach, "A person is obligated to say, 'The world was created for me'" (*Sanhedrin* 37a). "Be proud that you are created in the image of God. Taking pride in the greatness and exaltedness of your soul is not only proper, but obligatory. You are duty-bound to recognize your virtues and to live with this awareness" (Rabbi Avraham Grodzinsky, *Toras Avraham*, p. 28a).

completely free and independent.[12] A person who lacks self-control moves further away from his Creator and becomes an emotional junkie who depends on others to feed his fragile ego, and is a slave to his own impulses.[13]

Independence is not about being able to do whatever we like, whenever we like. Rather, it is about being able to do what we know is best for us. Imagine being on a diet and suddenly feeling the urge to eat a piece of chocolate. We fight the temptation, but eventually give in. Is this freedom or slavery? We felt like eating a piece of chocolate so we did. Did we like how we felt afterwards?

When we rise above our inclinations and resist them, we exercise self-control and thus experience true freedom. As our Sages remind us, "Who is strong? One who controls his (natural) inclination."[14]

The Paradox of Respect

The people who crave the most respect are the ones who are least likely to get it. In an attempt to garner recognition, people with low self-esteem do the very things that make other people lose regard for them. They brag about themselves and are arrogant. They are quick to

---

12. That man resembles God, in having free will, is the interpretation according to the Rambam, *Hilchos Teshuvah* 5:1, and many other commentators.

13. "Those who are in control of themselves recognize that they are not in control of the world, and are therefore liberated from worry. Moreover, exercising self-control offers solace, since we are cognizant of the fact that we have done as much as we can, and trust that God will take care of the rest. Those who lack self-control mistakenly believe that they are in control of their circumstances, and therefore easily become neurotic, angry, and frustrated." D. Lieberman, *Real Power* (Viter Press, 2008) p. 86.

14. *Pirkei Avos* 4:1.

judge, gossip, criticize, and embarrass others. But no one respects someone who puts people down and who is constantly seeking the approval of those around him. Fittingly, we learn, "Who is honored? He who honors others" (*Pirkei Avos* 4:1). The Sages further teach us that: "One who *runs away* from honor will find honor chasing after him. One who *chases after* honor will find honor running away from him" (*Eruvin* 13b).[15] Ironically, not only do others think less of the egocentric person but he also winds up feeling worse about himself. Since we gain self-respect by making good choices, this behavior further injures his feeling of self-worth.

Smoke and Mirrors

When a person suffers from very low self-esteem, it does not matter how accomplished he appears, he is dependent upon everyone and everything to boost a faltering self-image. In *Megillas Esther*, we are introduced to the wicked Haman. His behavior exemplifies the egocentric mindset. Haman had money, power, and prestige, yet became enraged when a single person, Mordechai, failed to show him respect. [16]

Do not fall into the trap of believing that a person with an inflated ego likes himself; ego and self-esteem are inversely related. No matter how much a person appears to be happy with himself, if he is egocentric, that person is miserable. This

---

15.   A man complained to Rabbi Simchah Bunim of Parshischo, "The Talmud states that when a person runs away from honor, honor runs after him. I run away from honor, but honor does not pursue me." "The reason," explained the Rabbi, "is because you keep looking over your shoulders and it hides from you" (*Simchas Yisrael*, p. 57).

16.   *Esther* 3:2-6.

statement is not conjecture, but a law of human nature—it is psychological math.[17]

Evaluating a person's degree of self-esteem is not difficult, but it can be perplexing if you do not know what to pay attention to and what to ignore. Here are five main misconceptions that will help us understand the behavior of people in our lives, as well as reveal insights into our own behavior.

Observation 1: Self-Esteem Versus Confidence

Self-esteem is often confused with confidence, but the two are quite different, and the distinction is important. Confidence is how effective we feel within a specific area or situation, while self-esteem is defined as how much we recognize our inherent self-worth and know that we are precious in the eyes of God.[18] Simply, we can feel good about ourselves yet not feel optimistic that we will succeed in certain situations.

For instance, a man who has high self-esteem may be a poor chess player, but he likes himself. He will exhibit signs of decreased confidence when playing with a superior player, yet his self-worth remains unaffected. (A person's confidence in a particular situation is rooted in a variety of factors: previous performance, experiences, feedback, and comparisons.)

Self-esteem can affect confidence. Studies show for instance, that the greater a person's self-esteem, the more inclined he is

---

17. W. Rowatt, C. Powers, V. Targhetta, J. Comer, S. Kennedy, & J. Labouff, "Development and Initial Validation of an Implicit Measure of Humility Relative to Arrogance." *The Journal of Positive Psychology* 1 (2006), pp. 198–211.

18. We previously defined self-esteem as self love. Our understanding is easily reconciled because poor choice leads to an egocentricity which blocks our ability to recognize God in our lives, and to feel His love for us.

to feel comfortable in a new situation.[19] However, the opposite is not true.

A person who desires to have a greater sense of self-worth, and attempts to do so by placing great emphasis on a specific trait, may exhibit signs of higher self-esteem to the untrained eye. However, a person's feelings of self-worth are shaped by one's free-will behavior, rather than the assets at one's disposal. Therefore, what we may perceive as self-esteem is really an inflated sense of confidence confined to a God-given talent.

Observation 2: The Success Story

We cannot gauge a person's self-esteem by how successful he is, because society's idea of success may be radically different from our own.

For example, a partner in a major law firm may appear to be successful to the casual observer, but if his lifelong dream was to do something else, and he abandoned this dream to appease others, or to garner their respect, he quite possibly will have low self-esteem because his decision was motivated by fear. Conversely, an artist with little money may not be the traditional notion of success, but if he is fulfilling his true desire, then he may enjoy high self-esteem, because he is proactively moving his life in the direction of his choosing.

If any of our objectives hinge on outside approval or acceptance, we will never be independent, and we will always look to the rest of the world for emotional reinforcement.

---

19.   A. M. Lane, L. Jones, M. J. Stevens, "Coping with Failure: The Effects of Self-Esteem and Coping on Changes in Self-Efficacy," Journal of Sport Behavior 25 (2002), pp. 67–69.

Observation 3: Humble or Weak?

It is easy to mistake humility for weakness, when in fact humility is synonymous with strength. When a person acts with humility, he is fulfilled. That person is not occupied with doing things that make an impression, but is free to do *what is right*. This is the gateway to self-esteem and to emotional freedom.

The difficulty lies in knowing whether a person is genuinely humble, or is *acting* humble as a way of getting other people to like him. The ability to discern one's nature is within our grasp. Rabbi Moshe Chaim Luzzato writes: "A person who is not sincerely humble, but only acts as if he had humility, will not be able to hide his arrogance. Eventually it will become visible to others."[20]

A secondary agenda may lie behind the humble mask. Perhaps this person acquiesces to the wishes of others, not because he wants to do good, but because he is afraid to say no, or does not feel worthy of asserting himself. Clearly, it is important to distinguish between those who are genuinely humble and possess high self-esteem and those who allow themselves to become prey.

Observation 4: Self-Esteem Versus Mood

Generally speaking, self-esteem coincides with a more pleasant and positive demeanor; but it is difficult to gauge a person's self-esteem by his current disposition. A person may appear to be in a good mood, and is outgoing, engaging, and warm. However, in actuality this person may be a self-absorbed narcissist who for a short span of time merely adopts this persona.

---

20.   Rabbi Moshe Chaim Luzzato, *Mesilas Yesharim*, ch. 11 & 22.

Observation 5: A Thimble or a Bucket?

We cannot evaluate a person's self-esteem by how righteous or good he appears to be. Each person is born with different God-given potential. A person who seems to be selfish may be working as hard as he can to be more giving, and therefore will feel genuinely good about himself (as a result of doing his best with the tools at his disposal).

Conversely, a person who appears to be virtuous may in actuality, not be doing enough according to *his* potential, and as a result, his conscience gnaws at him, and he suffers from low self-esteem. [21]

Imagine a thimble and bucket each filled with a liquid. The thimble feels as full as the bucket. Can we say that the bucket is fuller than the thimble? In relative terms, the bucket has more liquid; in absolute terms, they are each full. The same can be said for human beings.

We stand on an never-ending ladder whose starting point is irrelevant. We might be capable of climbing easily, but choose to be complacent and climb only a few rungs at our leisure. Genuine progress (and therefore self-esteem) is recognized only through looking at our effort in relation to our

---

21.   While the choices we make throughout our lives have a profound impact on our emotional stability, mental health disorders result from a combination of factors—genes, neurochemistry, personality, environmental stressors, childhood traumas, and other developmental factors. And although there is no discounting the power of exercising our free will and its influence on every aspect of our lives, a person's emotional instability may be partly attributed (or in rare instances, even entirely) to aspects beyond his control. In Chapter 24 we discuss that an adult's self-esteem may be damaged through lack of love or intense turmoil experienced at an early age.

ability.[22] Our Sages teach us: "Do not judge your fellow until you are in his place."[23] Since each person is at his own level, it is impossible to ever judge another person as we can never really stand in his place.

How Can We Tell How Much Self-esteem a Person Has?

The gauge of another's self-esteem is seen as a reflection of how he treats himself and others. The *Baalei Mussar*[24] teach that the test of a person's spirituality is how he regards other people. On the flip side, Hillel reminds us, "If I am not for myself who will be for me? If I am only for myself, what am I?"[25] The synthesis of these two insights reveal our answer.

A person who lacks self-esteem may indulge excessively to satisfy only his own desires, while not treating others particularly well (a product of an arrogant mentality). Or this person may devote significant time and energy to gaining the approval and respect of others, to the extent that he fails to take care of his own needs (a product of the doormat mentality). A person with high self-esteem strikes the balance between giving both to himself and to others.

$\sim$

22. When we become frustrated by a lack of clear success, we mistakenly believe that we are in control of our circumstances—deluded by our ego which is outcome-oriented and equates success with a visible payoff.

23. *Pirkei Avos* 2:4.

24. Masters and teachers of the Mussar movement.

25. *Pirkei Avos* 1:14.

Understanding where a person is coming from not only helps us feel compassion, but is useful in finding the most appropriate strategy when dealing with an interpersonal conflict. Of course, recognizing how our own ego and sensitivities warp our world helps us to reevaluate our concerns, and perhaps dismiss some that are products of our own insecurities.

Overcoming
Personality Conflicts

Whether you are seeking to improve a relationship with a friend, family member, or co-worker, the following principles show us how to change the foundation of a relationship, and enhance the way you interact and communicate.[1]

Rule 1: Express Respect

Many personality conflicts arise as a result of feeling disrespected. You may have unintentionally not given this person your full attention, or he misinterpreted a look or something you said or did. It doesn't take much for a person with low self-esteem to determine that a person doesn't like him.

---

1. "It is our responsibility to perceive the wider reality, which is that God is speaking to us through every person and situation. Relationships are a very common area in which people often miss the message and focus on the messenger. God does not need us to solve another person's problems—He is perfectly capable of solving them Himself. On a simple level, it is true that we should help others, but we must also understand the larger picture and ask ourselves the important question, 'What lesson can I learn from this person?'" See D. Lieberman, *Real Power* (Viter Press, 2008) pp. 107–108.

This is true for all of us, to some degree. There are aspects of ourselves that we dislike, and we project our own disdain of these qualities into the minds of others. We believe, albeit unconsciously, that others must see these faults and dislike us as well.

"And you rebelled in your tents and you said, 'It is for God's hatred of us that He brought us out of Egypt to destroy us.'"[2] Rashi explains this concept stating that: ". . . it is not He who hated you, but (rather) you who hated Him."[3] In psychological terms this is called *projection*. We project our feelings on to the other person and believe that he feels as we do.

As one of the great *Mussar* leaders has observed, when a "taker" sees other people do completely unselfish acts he simply does not believe what he sees. He insists on calculating and speculating what selfish ends these apparently unselfish acts must serve. It is obvious to him that everyone must be like himself."[4]

An effective method to show someone that you hold him in esteem is to tell a third party,[5] maybe a mutual friend,[6] what it is that you genuinely *like* and *respect* about this person or how you

---

2. *Devarim* 1:27.

3. Rashi, ad loc.

4. See Rabbi Eliyahu Dessler, *Michtav m'Eliyahu*, vol. 1, *Kuntres HaChessed*, pp. 32–51. Hereafter, "*Kuntres HaChessed.*"

5. You may be thinking, "Why can't I just go and tell him myself? Why this cloak-and-dagger act with a third party?" If you tell him yourself, you run the risk of him thinking that you're being insincere or patronizing. When he hears the message from a third party he is friendly with, his ego is not on alert.

6. Choose a friend who also has positive feelings for the person you're describing. Do not choose an enemy of the person you're complimenting (or even one with a less-than-positive assessment of him). He might undermine the intended compliment and speak *lashon hara* (forbidden speech). Complimenting someone in the presence of his enemy is *avak lashon hara* in any case (i.e., speech that can be taken negatively or cause others to speak negatively about another person). (Cf. Rambam, *Hilchos De'os* 7:4; *Sefer Chafetz Chaim, Hilchos Lashon Hara* 9:1).

commend him for something he's done or even stands for. Once the person sees that we admire him, the barriers of hostility will begin to break down. After all, it is hard to dislike someone who not only likes us but *respects* us as well.

Have you ever had the experience of having someone whom you don't particularly like, pay you a huge compliment? Or ask your advice? Suddenly you find yourself forced to reevaluate your feelings toward that person and adjust them to be more favorable. We would rather adjust our thinking of him than believe that his high opinion of us is flawed.

This form of appreciation is known as *reciprocal affection*. We tend to like someone once we are told that they have the same feelings for us.

Along these lines, "A person's honor should be dear to you as your own."[7] Do not make any gesture or comment that indicates a lack of respect. Specifically, when he's speaking to you, give him your undivided attention.[8]

Being half-listened to, or perhaps, more accurately, half-ignored does not cultivate warm feelings towards the other. Perhaps you've had the experience of conversing with someone at an event when you suddenly become aware that his eyes are roving the room behind you, even as he's pretending to be listening to you.

Listening—really listening—is about respect. If someone is talking to you, it's disconcerting to listen with one ear or keep

---

7. *Pirkei Avos* 2:10. The core of interpersonal success lies in giving honor to others; while the foundation of personal growth lies in forgoing our own honor, and bestowing it upon others.

8. Imagine having a conversation with someone during which time, his phone rings constantly, but he chooses not to answer it. Perhaps you even say, "Do you need to get that?" But he simply says, "Don't worry about it. I'm interested in talking to you right now." Wouldn't this make you feel good?

one eye trained on the clock, computer, or newspaper. It might seem trivial, but this type of consideration for another person's feelings significantly impacts on a relationship.

From the Heart

In the days of Rabbi Chaim of Volozhin (a noted disciple of the Vilna Gaon), it happened that a butcher became very angry at the Rabbi of his city for rendering a decision that the meat of a cow the butcher wanted to sell was not kosher. The decision cost the butcher a great loss. In his rage, the butcher devised a scheme to murder the Rabbi. On a pretext, he had the Rabbi travel with him on a lonely road. Along the way, the butcher took out his sharp knife and wanted to kill the Rabbi. When the Rabbi saw that nothing he could say would make a difference, he started to mentally focus on all of the positive qualities and attributes of the butcher. Suddenly, there was an astonishing transformation. In the midst of the Rabbi's thinking about the virtues of the butcher, the butcher changed his mind. With a strong feeling of love, the butcher—with tears in his eyes— kissed the Rabbi and begged his forgiveness.[9]

Rule 2: Allow Him to Give to You

We tend to believe that the way to get people to like us is to do nice things for them. Although this is true, the reality, however, is that people actually like us even more when they do something for *us*.

---

9. Rabbi Chaim Zaitchyk, *Ma'ayanei HaChaim*, vol. 3, p. 191.

This is for three reasons:

1 Whenever human beings invest time, energy, and attention in anything, in this case a person, the result is that they feel closer and more attached to the recipient of their attention. Every positive emotion stems from giving and flows outward from us to others, whereas every negative emotion revolves around taking for selfish motives.[10] Aptly, the root of the Hebrew word, *ahavah*, love, is *hav*, to give.

An Excerpt from Benjamin Franklin's Autobiography:

> My first promotion was my being chosen, in 1736, clerk of the General Assembly. The choice was made that year without opposition; but the year following, when I was again propos'd (the choice, like that of the members, being annual), a new member made a long speech against me, in order to favour some other candidate. I was, however, chosen, which was the more agreeable to me, as, besides the pay for the immediate service as clerk, the place gave me a better opportunity of keeping up an interest among the members, which secur'd to me the business of printing the votes, laws, paper money, and other occasional jobs for the public, that, on the whole, were very profitable.
>
> I therefore did not like the opposition of this new member, who was a gentleman of fortune and education, with talents that were likely to give him, in time, great influence in the House, which, indeed, afterwards happened. I did not, however, aim at gaining his favour by paying any servile respect to him, but, after some time, took this other method. Having

---

10. Rabbi Eliyahu Dessler, *Kuntres HaChessed*, pp. 35–38.

heard that he had in his library a certain very scarce and curious book, I wrote a note to him, expressing my desire of perusing that book, and requesting he would do me the favour of lending it to me for a few days. He sent it immediately, and I return'd it in about a week with another note, expressing strongly my sense of the favour. When we next met in the House, he spoke to me (which he had never done before), and with great civility; and he ever after manifested a readiness to serve me on all occasions, so that we became great friends, and our friendship continued to his death. This is another instance of the truth of an old maxim I had learned, which says, "He that has once done you a kindness will be more ready to do you another, than he whom you yourself have obliged." And it shows how much more profitable it is prudently to . . . return, and continue inimical proceedings.[11]

2 When we allow others to give, they feel better about themselves, since giving reinforces the feeling that we are in control and independent.

3 Helping others engages a psychological phenomenon called *cognitive dissonance*, whereby the giver concludes— partly unconsciously—that he must like the recipient of his kindness. Otherwise, he would be helping people he does not even like.[12]

There is no greater way to bond with someone than by allowing him to be a part of your life and give to you. Ask this person for

---

11.   A year after Benjamin Franklin's death, his autobiography, entitled *Memoires De La Vie Privee*, was published in Paris in March of 1791.

12.   From a Torah standpoint, such behavior is commendable; but if he were on this level, it is likely you would not be having these difficulties with him in the first place.

advice and input whenever you think he might have something worthwhile to contribute.

Rule 3: Show Your Human Side

We should never be afraid of responsibly opening up ourselves to the people in our lives. When we show our vulnerability, the wall of separateness dissolves and compassion emerges; the other is then driven to respond to your needs as if they were his own.

Often, in an attempt to get someone to like us, we'll employ what is called *self-enhancement behavior*. This is when we tell and show the other person how accomplished and wonderful we are, so that he will come to like us. Yet when you're dealing with a person who is insecure and feels threatened, findings clearly indicates that *self-deprecating* behavior is the optimum attitude.[13] This would mean offering information about yourself that *isn't* flattering. It shows humility, honesty, and trust—three traits that help provide a successful resolution to any personality conflict.

Rule 4: Like Attracts Like

The *Baalei Mussar* teach that the essence of love is similarity. When we say that people love each other, the concept is that they view themselves as having much in common in their character, traits, and temperaments. This unites them; and when there is this unity, we say that one person feels love for the other.

---

13.   E. Aronson, B. Willerman, and J. Floyd, "The Effect of a Pratfall on Increasing Interpersonal Attractiveness," *Psychonomic Science* 4 (1966), pp.227–228.

Contrary to popular opinion, research in human behavior confirms that opposites do not attract.[14] We may find someone interesting because of how different he is from us, but we actually connect more with people who are similar to us and have similar interests.

Analogous to this law is the principle of "comrades in arms." People who go through life-changing situations together tend to create a significant bond. For instance, soldiers in battle or those in fraternity pledge classes who get hazed together usually develop strong friendships.

It's for this reason that two people who have never met but who have shared a similar previous experience—whether it's an illness or winning the lottery—can become instant friends. *Like attracts like.* When you speak to this person, talk about what you both enjoy and what you have in common.

Rule 5: Show Genuine Enthusiasm When You Greet the Person

Psychologist Daniel Goleman writes: "It happens that smiles are the most contagious emotional signal of all, having an almost irresistible power to make other people smile in return."[15] Our Sages echo this point: "Showing the white of your teeth to a fellow man is more beneficial than offering a glass of milk."[16]

---

14.   D. W. Nangle, C. A. Erdley, K. R. Zeff, L. L. Stanchfield, and J. A. Gold, "Opposites Do Not Attract: Social Status and Behavioral-style Concordances and Discordances Among Children and the Peers Who Like or Dislike Them," *Journal of Abnormal Child Psychology* 32 (2004), pp. 425–435.

15.   Daniel Goleman, *Social Intelligence: The New Science of Social Relationships* (Bantam Books, 2006).

16.   *Kesubos* 111b.

The Sages stress the significance of ensuring that our initial contact with a person be as pleasant and gracious as possible: "Be the first to greet every person,"[17] "Greet every person with a pleasant countenance,"[18] and, "Greet every person with joy."[19] They wish to convey that receiving people with zeal not only helps to make them feel good about themselves, but also about you, the source of their warm feelings.

The importance of immediately setting the right tone cannot be overstated. In every type of relationship, whether you are returning home to your spouse or greeting a long-lost friend, those initial few moments of interaction will dramatically shape the quality of your encounter.

Indeed, *Chazal* say, "Everything goes after the beginning." This is why people are very careful with their behavior on Rosh Hashanah (the Jewish New Year), so that their entire year will reflect their intentions at this time. Greet with a warm smile, and it will set an upbeat tone for the rest of the conversation.[20]

Rule 6: Give Him the Benefit of the Doubt

Dan le'kaf zechus, "judging favorably," is a Torah concept and a mitzvah with vast implications.[21] If he borrows something

---

17. *Pirkei Avos* 4:15.

18. *Ibid.* 1:15.

19. *Ibid.* 3:12.

20. *Modeh Ani* is the prayer we say upon opening our eyes each morning. The classic translation is: "I offer thanks to You, O living and everlasting King, for having restored my soul within me; great is Your faithfulness." By beginning the day with thoughts of appreciation and gratitude, we set a positive and productive tone for the day.

21. *"B'tzedek tishpot amisecha*—You must judge your fellow favorably." This is the positive mitzvah to judge one's fellow positively" (*Vayikra* 19:15). It obligates you

without permission or exits a meeting that you're conducting early and without explanation, let your first assumption be that he has a good reason. If you inquire about the incident, don't interrogate. Don't be accusatory or argumentative. Even if his motivation was less than pure, your reaction this time can change his actions the next time.

Rule 7: A Few Kind Words

It's amazing, but it seems that in all kinds of relationships, the only time we say something nice is when we've done something wrong. Be proactive from time to time. One nice word in the bank is worth a hundred after the fact. The Seforno (*Bamidbar* 22:6) comments on Balak's statement to Bilaam, "I know that when you bless it comes true." He says that Bilaam's only "talent" was the ability to curse (or more precisely he knew when to curse); but no one wants to see himself as a destroyer. When Balak adds "bless" into the mix, it flatters Bilaam, even though Bilaam knows that Balak doesn't even believe it to be true. But Balak knew something about human nature. Human beings are so thirsty for praise that even when we know it's insincere we still desire it.

In fact, research was done examining sixty-nine studies about influencing impressions and getting a person to like us. Of all tactics, the most successful was simply making the other person feel good about himself, whether through sincere flattery, compliments, or praise.[22] The bottom line is that

---

to formulate a plausible explanation to excuse a perceived insult from someone whose character you know (Introduction to *Sefer Chafetz Chaim*, Positive Mitzvah 3, *Be'er Mayim Chaim*, ad loc.; *Shabbos* 127a).

22. R. A. Gordon, "Impact of Ingratiation on Judgments and Evaluations: A Meta-analytical Investigation," *Journal of Personality and Social Psychology* 71

people crave to feel good about themselves and most people are forced to rely on others to sustain them.

An amusing anecdote is attributed to Rabbi Leib Chasman. A zealous person had burst into his synagogue and declared the Rabbi to be a *Lamed Vovnik*, one of the thirty-six righteous people who perceive the Divine Presence on a daily basis.[23] Afterwards the Rabbi acknowledged that even though he knew these were false words spoken by an ill person, *it still felt good!*

The Torah forbids insincere flattery. Be certain then, that you have the right motivation. Rabbi Eliyahu Dessler distinguishes between flattery and respect: "To flatter is to show respect towards someone only in order to get something from him in return. A person who has the attribute of wanting to do acts of kindness, on the other hand, will want to do and say things to honor others out of a sincere desire to give the other person pleasure."[24]

Rule 8: Join Sides

If you learn that this person has made a mistake, reassure him that it could happen to anyone, and tell him he shouldn't be so hard on himself. Whatever you do, don't criticize or condemn. In a situation where he's having a disagreement with another person (which likely happens often), defend him, if you believe there's any merit to his side of the argument.[25] When the two

---

(1996), pp. 51–70.

23.   Cf. *Sukkah* 45b.

24.   Rabbi Eliyahu Dessler, *Kuntres HaChessed*.

25.   Ideally one should try to make peace between the arguing parties. But if one's aim is simply to be supportive, then one should be very careful only to defend him regarding the issue at hand (e.g., that she was wrongfully overcharged) but

of you have a disagreement, you don't win anything by proving that you're smarter than he is. Whereas, if you acknowledge that he's made an insightful or interesting point—even if you have to disagree—you have everything to gain.

Rule 9: Kindness Overload

Sometimes the source of conflict is rooted in something deeper: ideals. Why are we sometimes angered by beliefs or values that are different from our own?[26] Basically, we live our lives in certain ways, according to our value systems and our set of rules and conduct. When we encounter a person whose beliefs oppose ours, we either (a) become threatened out of fear that we may be wrong, or (b) become concerned that the other person's values will have a negative impact on himself, ourselves, or on those whom we care about.[27]

---

not defend her regarding unrelated personal issues (e.g., that the other person is miserly and unfriendly). This is the difference between a *dispute*, which is not, strictly speaking, prohibited and a *machlokes*, which is prohibited. Briefly, a *dispute* revolves around a difference of opinion or attitude; but once it becomes personal the situation enters the realm of a *machlokes* (literally, 'a division') (*Kodesh Yisrael*, ch. 25).

26.   While it is common to disagree over certain subjects, and even to avoid a relationship with someone because his beliefs violate your perception of what is right, feeling actual anger at someone for holding an opposing view is neither healthy nor productive. In almost every instance, the Torah advises us that moderation is the rule—with one exception: arrogance and anger. "If one is a wise man, his wisdom leaves him; if he is a prophet, his prophecy leaves him. The life of the irate is not true life . . . one should distance himself from anger and accustom himself not to feel any reaction, even to things which provoke anger. This is the good path." (Rambam, *Mishnah Torah, Hilchos De'os* 2:3). "When a person gets angry he loses control, and loses his wisdom" (*Pesachim* 66b).

27.   Other mitigating causes include: guilt, resentment, shame, envy, and embarrassment.

Objecting to a person's behavior does not usually give one the psychological permission to sever the relationship, or to harbor hate for the person. But the reason the relationship suffers is because of the way the two parties treat each other as a result of this initial dispute. Invariably, with each disrespectful comment or disapproving glare, each side feels even more justified in disliking the other, and it is this cycle of disrespect that gives way to ingrained hostility.

It is for *this* reason that these types of personality conflicts are often so difficult to resolve. The original cause of the conflict could be navigated or even forgotten, but because of the charged atmosphere, the two parties allow their relationship to deteriorate near to the point of no return.

Even if much time has passed, you can still reverse the slide by showing complete respect *in spite of* the others' comments and attitude.[28] This method engages two principles.

The first one, which we discussed earlier is *cognitive dissonance*: an uncomfortable emotional tension which arises from holding two conflicting thoughts at the same time.

If you're treating a person well in spite of how badly he's treating you, then he has to reconcile why it is that he's being unpleasant to somebody who is kind and respectful to him. In order to justify this contradiction, the person naturally eliminates one of the elements of the equation. He needs to

---

28. This certainly does not mean that you should allow yourself to be a verbal punching bag, but you may find that if you demonstrate respect, his behavior will, over time, begin to realign itself to be more accepting. If an estrangement exists and there is no direct contact, then these feelings may be conveyed through letters, tapes, or messages from mutual friends and relatives. In fact, if you don't feel that you can do this in person, from an emotional standpoint, a handwritten note is at times equally effective and in some cases more so. The person can read your note again and again, letting it sink in, and you avoid a potentially unproductive face-to-face confrontation.

unconsciously resolve the contradiction—if you're such a bad person, why are you so kind and good to him? One of his beliefs will have to budge. With polite persistence on your part, he will often be moved to conclude that you must be a good person who holds a flawed belief instead of a bad person whom he would likely want nothing to do with.

This approach also activates what is called *guilt reduction.* Studies show that a person will do almost anything to ease feelings of guilt.[29] When you're treating the other person kindly, and he's treating you poorly, he will, on some level, feel awkward. In order to reconcile these feelings, he will (hopefully) opt for the path of least resistance and change his behavior to one that is more tolerant.

In reality, many people have friendships and relationships with people whose beliefs are fundamentally different from their own. The secret is to stay away from these contentious subjects. Not every issue needs a thorough, complete, and intensive investigation. If you want to find something to argue about, you will have no shortage of topics.

Real-Life Scenarios

If you are experiencing a personality conflict with someone, turn to a mutual party and relay what you genuinely admire about the person with whom you are having difficulty. Follow this with a request for that person's help. This will also allow you to find out if the message was effectively relayed to him by

---

29. Two such studies include: D. J. Bem, "An Experimental Analysis of Self-persuasion," *Journal of Experimental Social Psychology* 1 (1965), pp. 199-218; and J. Cooper, and R. H. Fazio, "A New Look at Dissonance Theory," in L. Berkowitz, ed., *Advances in Experimental Social Psychology* 17 (NY: Academic Press, 1984), pp. 229–266.

the mutual party, as he will then seek you out to help you with what you need.

A "I'm so impressed with the way Joseph dealt with the advertisers in the meeting. Do you think he'd give me some sales tips?"

B "I'm so proud of Ruth for sticking to her guns on that issue. I'd love to talk to her about how I can be more assertive."

C "Dr. Solomon is really someone I can count on for getting things done. Do you think he'd talk to some of the other doctors about time management?"

D "The way she keeps her home should be featured in a magazine. Do you think she'd give me some decorating tips?"

Then . . . when in conversation with the person with whom you are having difficulties, listen intently, ask questions, and talk about what you might have in common. Additionally, at an appropriate time, share something personal about yourself, even if it is mildly embarrassing.

"I ran into my neighbor and completely blanked on his name when I tried to introduce him to my friend." Or, "I was so absentminded; I walked right out of shul holding someone else's *siddur* (prayer book)."

When a personality conflict exists between two people, almost all interactions can potentially end in discord. However, when we are conscious of, and sensitive to, the reasons involved, we realize that beneath a person's challenging exterior lies the human desire to feel appreciated and respected. With such awareness, we are able to respond to the person with heightened sensitivity, and approach the situation from a place of compassion, rather than judgment.

3

Reject Advice Without Rejecting the Person

By definition, advice is something that is simply *offered*. Yet, have you ever wondered why it is that some people become infuriated when we don't take their suggestion? It happens because the person feels that it is not the *advice* that we are rejecting, but *him*.

Phase 1: Show Appreciation for the Input

Thank the person for his suggestion and tell him that you will think about it. Even if you disagree with him, and think it's a bad idea, allow him the dignity of feeling that you are going to consider his advice. (You may even be surprised to find that he is, in fact, right after all.)

Phase 2: Give Two Reasons Why You Agree and One Reason Why You Don't

A day or two after receiving the advice, offer him two reasons why he is right and then *one* reason why his idea doesn't make sense for you, at *this* time. Remember, he is not being paid for his advice, and is only trying to help. He only becomes upset if he feels ignored.

Phase 3: Thank Him for Getting You Thinking

Tell him that you've decided already to make *another change*, and it was thanks to his initial suggestion that you were inspired with this new idea. Now instead of feeling rejected, he feels part of the decision-making process.

Phase 4: Seek Out His Opinion on Something Else

Follow up by asking for his opinion on something else—related or unrelated to this situation. If at all possible, make sure that you ask him about something of minor significance, so that you can easily follow his suggestion. This solidifies for him the belief that you respect him, and that it was just one idea that you did not particularly agree with.

Real-Life Scenarios

A secretary suggests to her boss that it might be a good idea to redecorate the waiting area. She says, "Mr. Black, I think we would project a better image to our clients if we redid the lobby and made it more modern." Mr. Black, however, likes the Old World look and charm and has no desire to change it.

> Mr. Black: "That's an interesting idea, Ms. Green. Let me give that some thought." In most cases, Ms. Green, inspired by her boss's consideration, will continue to try to sell him on the idea.

[The next day] Mr. Black: "Ms. Green, I thought about what you said, and a more modern look might attract some people, and it would be nice to look at something different, but I think this motif projects a good image for us."

[After a brief pause] "But your observation got me thinking that we should make some changes around here and replace that sign on the door for one that's a little classier. Thanks a lot for your suggestion about how to improve things around here. Without it, the sign idea never would have occurred to me. Keep thinking! Oh, and also I wanted to get your opinion on something else. What do you think about giving the place a new paint job?"

He considered her input, and showed that he valued her and her idea. Think about how offended she might have been had he dismissed her suggestion out of hand.

When you're dealing with sensitive people (which applies to all of us at one time or another), this strategy may prove useful—especially when it spares another person's feelings. Furthermore, such an approach teaches us the value of truly considering others' opinions, without reflexively rejecting them.

In Business, Turn a Complaint into a Plus

W hen dealing with challenges at work, expressing frustration by rolling your eyes, tapping your foot, and crossing your arms may offer a degree of satisfaction, but you'll pay for it later.[1] When a customer, client, or patient complains about something trivial, he may have a legitimate grievance, but often the thought that stirs beneath the surface is that he unconsciously believes that he *deserves* to be treated poorly; and as he begins to question his self-worth he becomes increasingly agitated.

Whether the person's complaint is genuine or not, the following strategy can be utilized to ensure that the customer feels validated and valued.

---

1. If the person is hurt or embarrassed, then one may also be transgressing the prohibition against causing distress with one's words or actions (*Vayikra* 25:17). Our Rabbis tell us that causing distress verbally (*ona'as devarim*) is a more serious offense than taking money wrongfully through overcharging (*ona'as mamon*). Pain and insult cannot be undone once inflicted, whereas property or money taken wrongfully can at least be returned or repaid. In addition, verbally causing distress affects the victim directly, rather than through his possessions. In regards to causing distress verbally, the Torah reminds us, "You shall have awe of God" (*Vayikra* 25:17), but does not say this regarding taking money wrongfully (*Bava Metzia* 58b).

Phase 1: Simply Listen

Listen.[2] Don't agree or disagree. Even if the customer is partly to blame, resist the urge to tell him so. If you interrupt him while he's still upset, you risk him becoming more argumentative. As our Sages teach us: "Do not appease your fellow in the time of his anger."[3] Often, people need to express their feelings, and once they have done so, they are no longer as upset. By becoming defensive, and preventing the person from speaking, you are only fanning the flames of discontent.

Phase 2: Paraphrase Back

Once the person has finished speaking, paraphrase back what he has just said to show that you have been listening and that you acknowledge his complaint.[4]

Repeating a person's words initiates a subtle effect. When you mirror a person's words (or posture), that person sees a reflection of himself in you.[5]

---

2.   Our sages teach us there are seven traits that characterize a fool versus a wise man. Two of these traits are: "A wise man does not interrupt his fellow's words;" and "He does not hasten to answer" (*Pirkei Avos* 5:9).

3.   *Pirkei Avos* 4:18.

4.   A related *halachah* (Torah law) regarding proceedings in a *Beis Din* (Jewish court of law) requires the *dayanim* (judges) to repeat back to each of the litigants their own arguments, as they had presented them. This is done in part to help the parties confirm that their position was heard and understood.

5.   See Robin Tanner and Tanya Chartrand, "Of Chameleons and Consumption: The Impact of Mimicry on Choice and Preferences," *Journal of Consumer Research* 34 (April, 2008), pp 754–766. These Duke University psychologists demonstrated how social mimicry can influence the behavior of a potential client or investor. Thirty-seven Duke students were asked to taste a new sports drink named Vigor and answer questions about the product. The interviewer mirrored the posture and movements of about half the participants. Participants who were

This effect has deep neurophysiological roots. According to University of Chicago neuroscientist Jean Decety, this rapport-building process activates brain circuits that are known to be involved in feelings of empathy. In fact, a similar empathetic neural response occurs when a person takes pleasure in the good fortune of a friend, or enjoys a conversation partner. "When you're being [mirrored] in a good way," states Decety, "it communicates a kind of pleasure, a social high you're getting from the other person."[6]

Phase 3: Ask Him for a Favor

Ask the customer to do something for you that shows you take what he said seriously. By doing so, you are conveying the message that you are *making his problem your problem*. For instance, a customer service agent might ask a client who was inadvertently overcharged on his invoice to look through previous statements to make sure that this was not a repeat occurrence.

Phase 4: Compensate

Let the customer know that you intend to compensate him for his trouble, without being specific how. You will notice that he quiets down quickly for several reasons. First, everyone likes

---

mimicked by the interviewer rated Vigor more favorably—and drank more of it—than participants who were not mimicked. The mimicked participants were also more likely to say they would buy Vigor, and to predict that it would be successful in the marketplace.

6.   A. N. Meltzoff and J. Decety, "What Imitation Tells Us About Social Cognition: A Rapprochement Between Developmental Psychology and Cognitive Neuroscience," *The Philosophical Transactions of the Royal Society* 358 (London, 2003), pp. 491–500.

to feel they are being compensated for their inconvenience. Second, he can't argue with you that he is not being adequately accomodated, because he doesn't even know what it is. And third, if it's something really great, he will not want to risk losing out on it by being too irate. Once he's more relaxed, you can better gauge the situation and decide on the appropriate action.

Phase 5: Now Explain

Up until this point, you have not offered an explanation. Now that you have neutralized his state, the person will be more inclined to listen and process objectively what you have to say in your defense.

It's interesting to note that research on corporate apologies looks at the question of attribution, suggesting the need for a clear cause of the harm with which an individual or company is associated.[7]

Mainly, your apology should be sincere and specific. It's been shown that giving a specific accounting of the circumstances involved, as opposed to vague generalities, is highly effective in reducing a person's annoyance.[8]

Further research details that the type of "why" makes all the difference. In an intriguing study of annual reports, researchers looked at how various companies—over a 21-year-period and across a range of industries—used the letter accompanying their annual report to explain company performance to their

---

7. M. E. Schweitzer, J. C. Hershey, and E. Bradlow, *Promises and Lies: Restoring Violated Trust* (Social Science Research Network).

8. D. R. Shapiro, E. H. Buttner, and B. Barry, "Explanations: What Factors Enhance Their Perceived Inadequacy?" *Organizational Behavior and Human Decision Processes* 1 (1992).

shareholders—and whether the type of explanation correlated to the company's stock price the following year.[9]

For the period studied—1975 through 1995—companies that took personal responsibility for a bad year realized better stock performance one year later (14%–19% higher) than did firms that blamed external, uncontrollable factors such as bad weather or the state of the economy.

When it comes to personal apologies, however, the psychology reverses itself. Research suggests that if your excuse is due to circumstances beyond your control, it is received much more favorably than an explanation that mentions only reasons that you had control over.[10]

For instance, if you missed an appointment, saying that, "I didn't feel up to it," or that, "I completely forgot," will likely generate unnecessary displeasure toward you. However, if a six-car pile-up on the freeway or a flat tire is the culprit, you will be more readily forgiven, because laying fault elsewhere *reduces* the extent to which the other party takes it personally.

Our ego, which looks to make everything that happens relate to us, is easily provoked in interpersonal relationships, while less of a factor in the impersonal corporate arena.

Above all, be honest. Even if the person does not like what you have to say, your truthfulness speaks volumes, communicating an important message: that you can be trusted. People would rather take their chances with someone who

---

9. L. Tiedens, C. Peterson, and F. Lee, "*Mea Culpa*: Predicting Stock Prices from Organizational Attributions," *Personality and Social Psychology Bulletin* 30:12 (2004), pp. 1–14.

10. B. Weiner, J. Amirkhan, V. S. Folkes, and J. A. Verette, "An Attributional Analysis of Excuse Giving: Studies of a Naïve Theory of Emotion," *Journal of Personality and Social Psychology* 52 (1987), pp. 316–324.

is principled than with someone who tells them what they want
to hear or who tries to cover up.

A Country Lawyer

Having never lost a single case, legendary trial attorney
Gerry Spence was hired to defend a man whose alleged
crime had been splashed across every newspaper in
town. An overwhelming majority of townsfolk had
already decided on his guilt. During jury selection, most
prospective jurors insisted that while they knew of the
case, they could nonetheless remain impartial. Given
the skewed media attention, the seasoned attorney
reasoned that these members of the jury pool were
probably disingenuous. He decided to take his chances
with a jury who felt his client was guilty and stated that
they could not be fair. Why? Because they were honest.
He had something to work with—people of integrity.
The verdict: not guilty on all counts.[11]

Real-Life Scenarios

As a hotel manager, you are confronted by a guest who was not
told until the next day that his urgent fax had arrived at the
front desk.

First, you listen intently without interrupting. And then you
paraphrase back what he's told you.

---

11.   G. Spence, *The Making of a Country Lawyer* (St. Martin's Press: 1996), p. 43.

"So, Mr. White, we had your fax sitting at the desk the entire time? I am terribly sorry. I'm so embarrassed that this happened to you. You have my complete assurance that I will be personally responsible for your comfort and needs during the rest of your stay. And I was wondering, sir, if you might do me a favor. The vice president of hotel operations may want to know what happened, directly from you. Do you think I could ask you to tell him yourself exactly what happened?"

[Toward the end of the discussion] "And I've thought of the perfect way to apologize appropriately. I want to do something special for you. I don't want to spoil the surprise, but I think you will enjoy it immensely."

Look what happened here. Mr. White was furious that nobody cared enough to tell him about his fax, and now *he's so important* that the vice president of the hotel may want to speak with him. It shows that they are taking him *seriously*, and that is what he wants. He's now probably thinking, "Wow, they sure are making a big deal about this little fax problem."

Studies reveal that a customer who has resolved a serious issue to his satisfaction will be more loyal to a company than a person who never had any complaints in the first place.[12] Moreover, it is estimated that it costs five times more to gain a new customer than to keep an old one. Expressed differently, if ten percent of customers who try your product or service can be turned into lifetime loyal customers, this can save a business, on average, up to eighty percent of what it would cost, from a marketing standpoint, to gain new customers.

---

12. F. F. Reichheld, "Loyalty-Based Management," *Harvard Business Review* 71 (March/April 1993), pp. 64–73.

When There's
Nothing Nice to Say

The Torah instructs us: *"Mi'dvar sheker tirchak"*—stay far away from lies and falsehoods.[1] However, under certain conditions it is permissible to withhold the entire truth, and in fact, one may even be obligated to do so, especially when it means that we can save a person's feelings.

The Chafetz Chaim defines *ona'as devarim* 'harmful speech' as the fourth form of *lashon hara* (gossip or slanderous speech which has the potential to cause any range of emotional, physical, or monetary damage). *Ona'as devarim* means causing pain with words, such as the often unintentional insensitivity at play when commenting on a person's spouse, new circumstance, purchase, and so on.

If a person asks for your thoughts about something *after the fact*—meaning there is nothing that can be done—*give him approval and assurance*. It's what he's really asking for anyway.[2]

---

1. *Shemos* 23:7

2. The following is based on *Hilchos Bein Adam l'Chavero*, by Rabbi Yitzchak Berkowitz: Inconsequential falsehood (i.e., a 'white lie' that causes no harm to anyone) is permitted. Indeed, one may even be obligated to use a white lie for the sake of forging peace between enemies, brothers or a married couple (Cf.

Imagine the following scenario: an acquaintance asks your opinion on his new custom-made suit. In truth, he is not asking you for your opinion—he's asking for a compliment or a confirmation of the fact that he has made the right choice. If he truly wanted your opinion, he would have brought you swatches of fabric so you could help him decide.

In addition, if someone purchased an item that is unflattering or overpriced, and is unable to return it, we are not permitted to make any derogatory comments that show our disapproval of the purchase. Being brutally honest in a situation where the person is incapable of doing anything about it will only cause resentment and hurt feelings. In fact, Jewish law dictates that not only must we refrain from *criticizing* the purchase, but we actually have to *praise* the item to the buyer.[3]

However, if your friend is asking for your assistance so he can *avoid* making a mistake, then you have an obligation to be candid.[4] Therefore, when giving one's opinion, it is important to assess whether you are being asked for a kind word or for honest input.

Yevamos 65b; *Sha'arei Teshuvah* 3:181). Even in such cases, altering the truth carries a number of conditions, two of which are: (1) one may not alter the truth on a regular basis (*Yam Shel Shlomo, Yevamos* 6:46), and (2) it is prohibited to lie or alter the details of Torah law under any conditions (*Yam Shel Shlomo, Bava Kama* 4:9). When altering the truth in the interest of peace, the *halachah* also makes a fine distinction between a lie of omission—which is preferred—to an outright lie which is treated more stringently (*Chafetz Chaim, Hilchos Rechilus* 1:8).

3.   This is learned from the following Gemara: "Beis Hillel said to Beis Shammai, 'According to your view, if someone made a bad purchase in the market [and had no way of returning the item, but he still asked your opinion on the purchase], should you praise it in the purchaser's eyes or denigrate it? You would certainly say that one should praise it in his eyes. . .' " (*Kesubos* 17a).

4.   Assuming the comment does not constitute *lashon hara* about a third party. Nevertheless, certain situations, such as those involving business or dating, may follow a different *halachic* protocol—the details of which, are beyond the scope of this work.

In situations where you're sparing someone's feelings or avoiding embarrassment, it's perfectly prudent and proper not to be completely straightforward, as the Torah states, "You shall not hurt the feelings of one another, and you shall fear the Almighty."[5]

Rabbi Moshe Chaim Luzzato writes, "Your obligation when someone comes to consult you is to give him the same advice you would desire to hear if you were in his position. Focus only on the welfare of the person you are talking to and not on any personal benefit you might derive from giving him advice that is not in his best interest. If you are unable to do this, refrain from giving any advice whatsoever."[6]

Real-Life Scenarios

Questions that require a compliment or praise:

Q "What do you think of my daughter's piano playing?"
A "It's just lovely."
Q "How do you like my new patio furniture?"
A "It's beautiful."
Q "Isn't my wife a great cook?"
A "One of the best."

Questions that require the honest truth:

Q "We're thinking of naming our baby girl Sadie Sparky Woof Woof. What do you think?"

---

5. *Vayikra* 25:17.

6. Rabbi Moshe Chaim Luzzato, *Mesilas Yesharim*, ch. 11, based on the verse, "Do not place a stumbling block before the blind" (*Vayikra* 19:14), as explained by *Toras Kohanim Kedoshim* 2.

A   "I am not sure that's a great choice."

Q   "I have just been set up with someone who has been married six times, can't hold down a job, and has a self-portrait up in the post office."

A   "That doesn't sound like a good match for you."

Q   "I'm looking at a 1977 Ford Pinto for $40,000. Is that a good deal?"

A   "It doesn't sound like you're getting a great price. I would pass on it."

Although the above scenarios may seem obvious, it is important to remind yourself that unreserved honesty is not always the best policy. Doing what is right, however, is.

CHAPTER

6

How to Offer
Constructive Criticism

The Talmud says, "One who disparages does so from his own weakness."[1] Before we discuss strategies for how to offer constructive criticism, we must first question our motivation and ask ourselves if our assessment of this person is correct.

Rabbi Eliyahu Dessler writes, "When you see a fault in others, turn the thinking and analysis to yourself. Even if you don't share the fault in its entirety, you likely share it in some small measure. Even if your weakness has never manifested itself in action, you have most likely pondered doing the very thing you are criticizing."[2]

According to Chassidic teachings, the very reason that we are able to perceive the faults of others is because it lies within ourselves; it then vexes a person, who has not yet accepted this fault within himself or suffers from an overall sense of low self-esteem.[3]

---

1. *Kiddushin* 70a.

2. Rabbi Eliyahu Dessler, *Michtav m'Eliyahu*, vol. 5, p. 123.

3. *Meor Einayim, Likkutei Torah.*

Therefore, before voicing our criticism, we must make sure that we are not projecting our own disapproval of ourselves onto others.[4]

The Talmud elucidates that one of the reasons Jerusalem was destroyed was due to a lack of sufficient rebuke between people.[5] One must bear in mind though, that there's a right and wrong way to criticize, and your approach can make all the difference in the world. As you may have experienced yourself, sometimes you're open to criticism and other times, the slightest comment can send you crawling under the nearest rock or make you extremely defensive and argumentative. *What* you say, *how* you say it, *where* you say it, and *when* you say it all have a bearing on how your comments are received.

One Word

"Happen" is a remarkable word. When you insert this word into a sentence, it is difficult for the other person to get defensive because it downgrades your question from an answer-seeking inquiry or accusation to a mere curiosity. Note how the following sentences soften and become less confrontational with the introduction of this word.

- "Did you file the report?" versus "Did you happen to file the report?"
- "Have you been drinking tonight" versus "Did you happen to be drinking tonight?"

---

4. The famous psychiatrist and founder of Analytical Psychology, Carl Jung, once quipped: "Everything that irritates us about others can lead us to an understanding of ourselves."

5. *Shabbos* 119b.

• "Did you correct the invoices?" versus "Did you happen to correct the invoices?"

Type I: Indirect Criticism

A clever way to give criticism is *not* to criticize. Instead, offer praise while still accomplishing your objective. This method of indirect criticism minimizes the risk of the person taking your comments personally and also reduces the chances of him being offended.

Step 1: Lay the Groundwork

First, tell the person that you *really like, enjoy,* or *appreciate* him for the way he is or for what he does (focusing on the attribute or behavior that you want him to change).

Step 2: Reverse Course

After some time passes, tell the person that *you* have changed *your mind* and would like him to try a different approach. You can attribute your change of heart to new information you have discovered, or an article you just read—or perhaps simply the desire to try something different. In this way, the onus is on you. You are not blaming the person for doing something wrong, so he can't be offended. Rather, it's about *you* changing *your* mind. This request completely removes him—and hence his ego—from the equation.

Real-Life Scenarios

SCENARIO A: A newlywed husband doesn't like the way his wife makes his breakfast. The omelet is always too spicy. But he is afraid to tell her in case he hurts her feelings.

> Husband: "I really love your omelets . . . and I so appreciate that you take the time to make them for me."
> Wife: "Thank you!" [Some time passes—a day or so]
> Husband: [Before his wife prepares breakfast] "You know what, I was reading somewhere that spices can contribute to certain kinds of arthritis, and mine has been acting up lately. If you wouldn't mind, I would really appreciate it if you could prepare the omelets as you usually do, but without the spices. I know it won't taste the same, but if it helps my arthritis, it would be worth the sacrifice."
> [Afterwards] "Wow, I didn't think it could get any better, but it's even more delicious!"

Had he initially suggested that she change what she was doing, she might have been hurt. But because he first reassured her with praise, and his request had to do with *him* and not *her*, it was almost impossible for her to be offended.

I, Me, My

Wherever you can, use "I" statements. Instead of saying, "You didn't do this right," or, "You made a mistake," make it *your* issue: "I feel uncomfortable with this process," or, "I have a habit of doing it this way." This psychology is effective in a variety of situations. Let's say you're out shopping for a new bedroom set. When the salesperson tells you the price and you respond with, "Your price is too high," he will be forced to prove the quality and craftsmanship to you. If, however, you say something such as, "It's beautiful and well worth the money, it's just not within *my* budget," it then becomes you and he who together will try to figure out a way that you can buy the furniture; it's no longer he against you.

SCENARIO B: A school principal is concerned that her receptionist is slightly abrupt with the parents, and she would like her to be warmer and friendlier. Knowing how sensitive the receiptionist is, she feels she cannot be direct in her criticism.

Mrs. Harris: "You know, Sarah, I've been meaning to tell you that I received a nice compliment about how efficient you are with the parents."

Sarah: "Thank you, Mrs. Harris."

Mrs. Harris: [Later in the day] "Oh, by the way, I'm expecting Mrs. White to come by today to talk about her daughter. She may be a little uncomfortable, being that she's from out of town, so do me a favor and chat with her a little bit to make her feel extra welcome."

Sarah: "Of course."

Mrs. Harris: [Later that day, after the parent has left] "Sarah, I hope I am not driving you crazy, but it was obvious today how you put Mrs. White at ease. Do you think you could try this approach with other parents?"

Need an Opening?

What about those times when you want to bring up a subject that is delicate and personal, and are sure that it will cause offence? The best tactic is to ask him for advice on this very subject, or on behalf of a friend or relative. The conversation would proceed along the following lines: "Michael, I'd like your advice on something personal. Do you know how I can accomplish X? Or do a better job of Y? Or eliminate Z?" By adopting such an approach, you are providing an opening for the discussion, and he will perhaps examine himself and his own behavior, since he's the one giving you the advice. For instance, let's say that you have a friend who is a terrible gossip. The best way to broach the subject would be with the following opening: "Do you think I gossip too much? I've been trying to work on this. Any suggestions for me?" Now the conversation is far less likely to make him defensive, because he's not defending himself, he's only helping you. However, you are now able to more easily segue into a conversation about his behavior.

Type II: Direct Criticism

In matters of taste, opinion, and preference, the strategy for offering indirect criticism can be easily employed. However, when a person's behavior is objectively objectionable, bringing up the issue directly may be your best and only option. Naturally, we should exercise great caution to help ensure that your words are received in the way in which they are intended. Try to adopt as many of the following principles as possible:

1 According to the Ralbag, all rebuke should begin by admitting your own mistakes: "We find an example when Avigayil successfully calmed down King David, who was furious at her husband (I *Shmuel* 25:24–25). She began by admitting that she herself had made an error."[6]

When we openly acknowledge our own faults to the person we are criticizing, our humility then keeps the other's ego from engaging. Conversely, an attitude of self-righteousness will automatically galvanize the other's ego and he is likely to become defensive.

King Solomon echoes this thought in his deep insight into human nature: "Do not admonish the scoffer, lest he hate you; admonish the wise person, and he will love you."[7] According to Rabbi Moshe Alshich, this verse means to tell us that we are not speaking of two different people. Rather, there is a scoffer and a wise person within each of us. If you address the scoffer persona, he will resent your criticism and become angry with you; however, if you address his true essence— the soul—then he will welcome your words.[8] Who or what is the "scoffer?" The one whose *yetzer hara* or ego prevents him from listening to your points objectively. The wise person is he who listens with his *neshamah* (soul) and intellect, rather than with his emotions.

2 Let him know that the reason why you are approaching him at all is because you care about *him* and your *relationship*. Our Sages teach us that only sincere and heartfelt criticism has a chance of being effective. "Just as with water, the face (in the water) reflects the face (of the

---

6. *Ralbag*, ad loc.

7. *Mishlei* 9:8.

8. See *Rav Peninim* (Multitude of Pearls), on *Mishlei*, Venice, 1601.

observer), so too, is the heart of one person to another."[9]

3 According to Maimonides, one is obligated to offer constructive criticism privately.[10] Even if you are certain that the other person would not object to others hearing your comments, it is still advisable to speak to him behind closed doors. As we learn in *Pirkei Avos*: "Whoever shames another in public has no share in the World to Come."[11]

God told Moshe that the Jewish people should wage war against the people of Midian. Moshe then gives them detailed instructions on how they should wage this war. When they returned from the battle, however, Moshe learns that they failed to follow the specific plan that he had laid out for them: "Moshe . . . and all the leaders of the assembly went out to meet them outside the camp. Moshe was angry with the commanders of the army . . ."[12]

Even though Moshe was disheartened with those who were in charge of the battle, *he went out to meet them outside the camp* to deliver his reprimand in private.

4 Begin on a positive note. When God criticized Shaul, He praised him first.[13] Moshe Rabbeinu's rebuke of Klal Yisroel is another example of this rule. Rabbi Yeshaya Horowitz[14] explains that before beginning his criticism of the Jewish people, Moshe first emphasizes their

---

9. *Mishlei* 27:19.

10. *Hilchos De'os* 6:7.

11. *Pirkei Avos* 3:11.

12. *Bamidbar* 31:13–14.

13. See II *Shmuel* 21:1 and *Yevamos* 78b.

14. The *Shelah HaKadosh*, see glossary.

many good qualities and remarkable potential, which in turn paved the way for their receptivity to his critical message. Similarly, the Torah itself precedes the harsh warning of punishment with verses of blessing.[15]

5 Make sure to criticize the *act* rather than the person. In other words, instead of saying, "You're incompetent or reckless when you . . .", it's better to say, "You're such a wonderful person, and this behavior doesn't seem appropriate for someone of your refined character." Moreover, when referring to the act, it is not necessary to be explicit or spell out the exact transgression. Rashi, commenting on *Devarim* 1:1–5, explains that Moshe did not explicitly state the sins committed by the Jewish people over the past forty years in the Wilderness. Rather, he alluded to the people's transgressions in general terms only, "because of the honor of Israel." Later, Rashi quotes a *Midrash* that Moshe waited until the day of his death to rebuke the people, "lest they be ashamed," each time they saw him.[16] Indeed, Maimonides further points out: "Even when you rebuke someone privately, you should be very careful not to shame him."[17] If you know that the person will be embarrassed at the mere mention of his sin, even in private, you should simply hint at the sin and try to draw the person away from it.

6 Don't approach the conversation with the assumption that the person is deliberately and consciously acting inappropriately. It is best to presume that the mistake is unconscious, or that he is unaware of the perceived ramifications.

---

15. Cf. *Devarim* 28.

16. *Devarim* 1:5, according to *Ikkar Sifsei Chachamim*.

17. *Hilchos De'os* 6:8.

7 Share some of the responsibility if you can. You might say something such as: "I should have been more specific when we covered this . . ." This is, of course, more effective than: "I dislike it when you . . ."

8 Only offer criticism if you believe that there is a chance that the person will be receptive to your comments.[18] Also, you should be prepared to offer a solution. If you do not have a solution, then you shouldn't pursue this conversation in the first place. The purpose of rebuke is not to air your grievances, but to help the person you are criticizing find a constructive resolution.[19]

9 Criticism is most effective when you communicate the idea that he is not the first person to make this mistake. Whenever truthful, you can let the person know that you, too, once did or believed as he does, and you just found out that it is incorrect. You further sidestep his ego because you are coming into the conversation with humility—admitting your own lack of knowledge. For instance, "I had always thought that completely insulating hot food on Shabbos was not a problem, and I was just told that it may not be proper."

10 "The words of the wise, when spoken gently, are accepted."[20] The Rambam teaches that one should always offer criticism in a pleasant tone of voice."[21]

---

18. *Shulchan Aruch, Orach Chaim* 608:2; *Rema*, ad loc.

19. *Yevamos* 65b: "R' Illa said in the name of R' Elazar the son of R' Shimon, 'Just as there is a mitzvah for a person to say words [of reproof] that will be accepted, so too there is a mitzvah for a person not to say words [of reproof] that will not be accepted.' "

20. *Koheles* 9:17.

21. *Hilchos De'os* 6:7: "[You] should speak to him calmly and in a pleasant tone of voice . . . and inform him that [you] are only speaking to him [about the

Remember that your manner is as important as the content of your message; never bring up a sensitive topic if you are not in a kind and compassionate state. Rebuke delivered in anger will not be heeded.

11 The most important part of your overall strategy has to do with the timing of your conversation. The best time to talk is when you are removed from the event. For instance, if a Rabbi wants to let someone know that his conduct in the synagogue was disturbing and inappropriate, he should not do so in the synagogue, let alone during prayer.

Equally significant is putting time between the event and your criticism. By waiting a few days before verbalizing your criticism, you will reduce the person's ego attachment to the situation and he will be less sensitive to criticism. But the closer to the event (in both time and proximity) that you criticize, *the more he identifies* with his behavior and the more defensive he will become.[22]

12 Praise the slightest effort and improvement. Giving positive reinforcement for small successes will help to spur him on; at the same time, do your best to ignore minor setbacks. Studies show that even when our performance does not measure up to the positive feedback we receive, our confidence is nonetheless boosted and our performance in *subsequent trials* also improves.[23]

---

matter] for his benefit, in order to bring [your] friend to gain the rewards of the World to Come."

22. Another aspect to consider is that if you speak immediately, you might inject too much anger (and possibly frustration) into your tone, because you have not had a chance to calm down or formulate your thoughts in a more detached way.

23. K. A. Karl, A. M. O'Leary-Kelly, and J. J. Martocchio, "The Impact of

The opposite is also true: negative feedback adversely affects a person's performance.

Criticism, when offered and articulated correctly, can enhance our relationships, yielding positive benefits for all parties involved. However, before we choose our strategy and words, we need to look inward and examine our motives. Without substance and sincerity, our criticism is misplaced.

Can You Put Gloves On Please?

How do you *remind* someone to do something when you know that the mere act of *asking* is going to offend him? Tell the person that *you don't mind if he does it.* For instance, let's say that you're in a deli and the person behind the counter is not wearing gloves. He's handling money and wiping up the floor. Now he's about to make your sandwich. Asking him to please put gloves on shouldn't be offensive, but if you are concerned about his taking offense you could merely say, "Oh, you don't need to put gloves on if you don't want to." In which case he will probably put them on, as he wasn't "told to," but he knows that he is supposed to.

Feedback and Self-Efficacy on Performance in Training," *Journal of Organizational Behavior, vol.* 14 (1993), pp. 379–394.

How to Handle
Unfair Criticism

W hen we feel we are being attacked, our first reaction
is to protect ourselves and respond (or muse) harshly:
"How dare you talk to me like that!" Or "Don't you yell at me!"

But why let someone else dictate how you feel? Reacting in
anger gives another person control over your emotional state.
That's a lot of power for one person to possess, especially someone who is rude to you.[1]

---

1. Revenge and bearing a grudge are prohibited by the Torah (*Vayikra* 19:18).
Rashi (ad loc.) gives examples of each: *Do not take revenge*—[One man] said to
[another], "Lend me your sickle," [and the second] said to [the first], "No." The
next day [the second] said to [the first], "Lend me your axe," [and the first] said to
[the second], "I am not lending it to you, just as you did not lend me your sickle."
This is taking revenge. And what is *bearing a grudge*? [One man] said to [another],
"Lend me your axe," [and the second] said to [the first], "No." The next day
[the second] said to [the first], "Lend me your sickle," [and the first] said to [the
second], "Here it is for you, and I am not like you, in that you did not lend me
[your axe]." This is bearing a grudge (*Yoma* 23a), [The Hebrew word for grudge
(*situr*) shares its root with the Hebrew words for "keeping" or "guarding," (*netirah*)]
as he "keeps" the enmity in his heart even though he does not take revenge.

Regarding the prohibition of, "Do not take revenge and do not bear a
grudge" the *Orchos Tzaddikim* (*Sha'ar HaAchzarios*) comments: "Even if you are
tempted to take revenge from your enemies, [instead] work on developing your
positive attributes, and follow the path of the upright. This will be your revenge,
for your enemy will become distressed when he sees your pleasant manner and

If you resist your initial inclination to act defensively, you may be surprised at what happens. Instead of, "Why are you treating me like this?" try responding in the following non-confrontational way: "You seem to be having a rough day." Rather than a defensive response, such as, "I didn't do anything," or, "Don't speak to me like that!" try, "This seems to have upset you." Don't take possession of his problem. It's his problem, not yours.[2]

Sometimes criticism comes in the form of nicely packaged advice. In such a situation, thank the person for offering his insight, and then later you can decide whether or not there is any credence to his words. As expected, it can be hard to separate the message from the messenger, but when you do, you may find some good ideas. So even if you perceive the suggestion to be unhelpful, make sure you thank the person.

Recognize that if the advice given is intended to belittle rather than help, this person is coming from a place of pain. Instead of feeling self-righteous rage, demonstrate compassion

---

[that you maintain] your good reputation, and he will be dismayed upon hearing good reports about you. If, however, you take [revenge through] unpleasant steps, then your enemy will rejoice over the shame and disgrace you cause yourself, and in so doing it is he who has taken revenge from you."

2.   If the criticism is justified—even if poorly presented—there is a mitzvah to accept it and incorporate it into one's personality (Cf. *Sefer Mitzvos Ketanos*, *Mitzvah* 9, on the verse, "Remove the barrier of your heart and do not be stubborn anymore" (*Devarim* 10:16)).

There exists a natural inclination to reject constructive criticism, as Rebbi Tarfon said, "I wonder if there exists anyone in this generation who knows how to accept reproof. For if one says to [his fellow nowadays], 'Remove the splinter from between your eyes,' [i.e., refrain from a minor infraction, his fellow] will retort, 'Remove the beam from between your eyes' [i.e., refrain from a major transgression]" (*Arachin* 16b). Nevertheless, one of the forty-eight ways to acquire Torah wisdom is a love of criticism (Cf. *Pirkei Avos* 6:6).

and rise above it.[3] If you get upset, it's the same as kicking the shins of a 90-year-old man who wants to pick a fight with you. First, no matter what happens, you can't win. And second, what are you doing? Do not get defensive; and do not engage him. Take the advice of King Solomon who reveals: "A gentle response turns away anger; a negative response increases anger."[4]

This person is being disrespectful to you because he craves respect himself. By thanking him and asking him for his input, you feed his psyche and end the conversation.

Of course, not all criticism comes from people in pain; and just because his words are voiced in a harsh manner does not mean that this person doesn't care about you. It may be that his intentions are noble, but he lacks the skills to express himself effectively.

Real-Life Scenarios

Comment: "You know, Aharon, you were way off your game in that meeting."

Response: "Really? I'll have to review that later. You're so great for looking out for me. How would you have handled it?"

Comment: "Malka, you know that outfit is not very flattering on you."

---

3. While we may feel pained by someone who behaved wrongly, unquestionably, every bit of anger and negative emotion is tied into our ego. Theoretically, a person who has complete self-love would never be offended, hurt, or embarrassed in any situation. Through our egos, we connect the dots from another person's actions to a place of hurt. Regardless of what is said or done to us, the minute we move from compassion to anger or to any negative emotion, it is because we have made the situation about us, and now our ego takes over, and overtakes us.

4. *Mishlei* 15:1.

Response: "Oh, thanks for letting me know. I appreciate your honesty. You're such a special person. Where did you get such a great sense of fashion from?"

Comment: "I thought you were trying to lose weight. Do you think you should be eating that?"

Response: "Oh, you're so sweet for remembering that I'm dieting. Thank you. You seem to have great willpower. I'd love for you to tell me your secret."[5]

Alas, we should always keep in mind the optimum motivation for holding our tongue. The Talmud reveals that the strength of God is manifest through His non-reaction to the insults and blaspheming of the wicked.[6] Elsewhere, the *Midrash* states that one who is silent in the face of insults is called pious, and a partner with God. What greater motivation do we really need, to not return insults or criticism, after receiving them?

The next time someone fires a cheap shot your way, remember that, "Silence in the face of insult is a great virtue,"[7] and if you cannot muster the emotional strength to say, "Thank you," you can never lose by saying nothing at all. [8] Indeed,

---

5.   In such a situation, especially between two people who are close—such as two good friends or a husband and wife—it might be preferable that the wife tell her husband (using the strategy presented in the previous chapter) that although she appreciates him looking out for her, that it is difficult for her when he interferes in her diet, and that she prefers if he didn't comment on what she eats. By failing to express your true feelings, you are not enhancing the relationship, because deep down, you are hurt. If, however, your words will not be heeded, the appropriate response is to deflect the question and change the subject.

6.   *Gittin* 55b.

7.   *Orchos Tzaddikim, Sha'ar HaShtikah.*

8.   If this abusive behavior is a part of a larger pattern and you have an ongoing relationship with this person, you need to let him know that his behavior is

"The whole world exists only in merit of the one who bridles his mouth in a moment of strife."[9]

unacceptable and will not be tolerated. In such cases, silence is likely not to be the correct course of action, as a lack of assertiveness will perpetuate the cycle. At the same time, how one asserts himself often requires extreme delicacy, particularly where the other person may grow dangerously defensive. The need for responsible consultation or counseling is often required in such situations.

9. *Chullin* 89a.

Dealing with Emotionally Unstable Individuals

If someone in your life suffers from an emotional illness,[1] recognize that it is not your responsibility (nor is it likely within your ability) to cure the person—your emphasis should be on maximizing the potential of the relationship.

Once you come to terms with the reality of his condition and his limitations, it will be easier to accept this person into your life.

Just because two people are related, or have contact with each other, does not necessarily mean that they have a relationship, at least not in the traditional, healthy sense. A genuine relationship involves two people who give and take.[2]

---

1. In this chapter, we are discussing people who suffer from mental illness, whether or not they have been formally diagnosed. While we all see the world through a skewed lens, these people distort reality to a much larger degree—this is what makes it difficult to relate to them. Certainly, as people become less emotionally healthy, boundary problems invariably become more prevalent; those without a clear sense of self are naturally going to have an unclear sense of boundaries.

2. Not all people who give are givers. If a person sees himself as incomplete, he allows himself to be taken advantage of, to assuage feelings of guilt or inadequacy. He doesn't feel his needs are important enough and certainly not more

---

The reason that we become aggravated is because we mistakenly believe that we're in a relationship. If the other person is not capable of giving, then your expectations will routinely exceed the confines of his ability—and you will always be frustrated.

If instead, you reframe the dynamics and consider it *chessed* (kindness), then you will not rely on him to reciprocate your efforts or fulfill his obligations, according to the definition of a healthy relationship. Your attitude largely depends on your expectations. How you define it can make a huge difference in your way of thinking.

Don't Confuse Intelligence with Emotional Wellbeing

"But he's smart! Successful! Talented!" It is irrelevant. Intelligence is largely unrelated to self-esteem and emotional wellbeing. Moreover, research indicates that a person with a high IQ is not more inclined to be open-minded or able to weigh both sides of an issue.[3]

In any given situation, it is conceivable that a smart person can make a poor decision while his less intelligent counterpart can make a wiser, more thoughtful, choice. It is our self-esteem that largely determines the *direction* of our behavior, not our intelligence.[4]

---

important than others'. He is a quintessential people-pleaser, a perpetual door-mat, trying to please the world in a fruitless attempt to gain love and approval.

3.   D. N. Perkins, M. Farady, & B. Bushey, "Everyday Reasoning and the Roots of Intelligence," in J. Voss, D.N. Perkins, and J. Segal, eds., *Informal Reasoning* (Hillsdale, New Jersey: Lawrence Erlbaum Associates, 1991), pp. 83–105.

4.   The Hebrew word for *melech* (king) is understood as an acronym for *mo'ach* (brain), *lev* (heart) and *kaveid* (liver). A king must exercise great wisdom and self-discipline, and needs to be in complete control of these three organs. The order

An intelligent person has the *capacity* to make better choices, but his *desire* to do so is determined by his perception of reality. As we discussed, with high self-esteem, our ego is reduced, and our perspective expands; hence, we more readily see the truth beyond the illusion, where the right choice becomes the clear one.

Even so, we often persist in the belief that if we just present a rational argument and explain the facts clearly and logically, then this person cannot draw anything other than the right conclusion, and will then see things our way—the right way.

This thinking is more flawed than that of the person we wish to persuade—he cannot hear us.

We all have our blind spots: areas of life where we do not see what is obvious to others. It seems so ridiculous to us when others act irrationally, only because their blind spots are different than ours. We are just as irrational—more so, in fact—if we choose to not accept this fact, and instead become angry when another does not see our point of view.

The Vilna Gaon comments on *Mishlei*: "Answer a fool[5] according to his foolishness, lest he become wise in his own

---

of the words also alludes to a hierarchy of priorities. The brain or intellect must rule the heart, which represents emotions; and the liver which represents his base desires, must be subservient to his thoughts and feelings. When we lead with our emotions, our intellect supports our decision by distorting reality to reinforce our emotional conclusion. However, the Torah tells us—and life experience confirms— that the decision-making process should be intellectual, with one's emotions reinforcing the choice and infusing it with passion. This concept is expressed in the *Aleinu* prayer: "You are to know this day [the realness of God], and take to your heart that Hashem is the only God"—first we are to understand intellectually, and afterwards align it to one's emotions (as represented by the heart).

5. When we speak of a fool (*kesil*), we are not referring to someone who is mentally ill, but rather a person who, because of emotional issues, has difficulty in processing a situation rationally. Therefore, we may find an emotionally-based response to be more readily understood and accepted.

eyes."[6] He further states that, "It is important to remember not to reply according to your own logic, but in a way consistent with his distorted way of thinking in order to ensure that your communication will be accepted."[7]

To help enhance time spent with emotionally fragile individuals, incorporate the following two themes into the strategies presented in Chapter 2:

1. A Sense of Autonomy

Help him feel a sense of control in what he does and how he lives his life. In one study, residents of an old age home who were given more freedom—such as the ability to make strictly minor decisions, along the line of being able to choose meal options from a menu, instead of being served the "day's fare," and having the freedom to choose from several destinations for short outings—were not as prone to sickness, and the annual death rate *was cut in half*.[8]

If the opportunity to choose between stuffed cabbage and veal chops can dramatically increase the life span of an elderly person, imagine what autonomy can do for a person's emotional health.

---

6. *Mishlei* 26:5.

7. The Vilna Gaon in his commentary on *Mishlei* 26:5.

8. J. Rodin, "Aging and Health: Effects of the Sense of Control," *Behavioral Brain Research* (1994).

Sage Advice

Rabbi Abraham Twerski points out in his book, *Successful Relationships*, that the Torah says, "Assist him in doing it" (*Shemos* 23:5), which means that he does his share and you help him. He says that, "Doing things for others that they can do themselves unless there is a legitimate reason encourages them to be dependent. Much like a physical therapist who works with a patient to regain strength, we must not let this person's will atrophy."[9]

2. Connect to the Soul's Desire

Living contradictory to his values drains him. Such behavior forces him to justify his actions in a myriad of ways, but in the end this rationalization is exhausting.[10] It creates a division within him—an emotional battle. A person cannot simultaneously believe that X is all-important while spending his time, energy, and effort on Y. In order to remain emotionally solvent, he must live, at least to some extent, in accordance with his values and life priorities.

Encourage this person to be authentic in one area of his life, and then, in some small way, take steps to actualize the goal. If it was always his dream to be a painter, encourage him to buy paints and canvases; if he believes relationships are important

---

9. A. J. Twerski, *Successful Relationships: at Home, at Work and with Friends* (New York: Artscroll Mesorah Publications, 2003) pp.81–82.

10. "When a man transgresses and repeats the transgression, he deludes himself into believing that what he has done is permissible" (*Yoma* 87a). Subconsciously, however, tension between the truth and his behavior creates severe emotional turmoil.

(as the Torah tells us) have him forgive, or apologize to, someone with whom he is no longer in contact. Moving towards
something personally meaningful—and taking responsibility,
even with a single small step—will help to build one's emotional
strength.

Dr. Abraham Maslow coined the term "self-actualization" as
the pinnacle in the hierarchy of human needs, and summed up
the concept this way:

> "A musician must make music, an artist must paint, a
> poet must write, if he is to be at peace with himself.
> What a man can be, he must be. This is the need we
> may call self-actualization . . . it refers to man's desire for
> fulfillment, namely to the tendency for him to become
> actually in what he is potentially: to become everything
> that he is capable of becoming . . . "[11]

We said at the beginning of this chapter that our goal should
not be to try to cure or change someone who is mentally unstable; and the strategies provided here will not heal a person of
his emotional problems.[12] That being said, helping him to feel
better about himself *de facto* improves the relationship.

---

11.   A. Maslow, *Motivation and Personality* (NY: Harper, 1954), p. 46.

12.   If the person has the status of a sick person (*choleh*), then one is partly
fulfilling the mitzvah of caring for the sick (*bikkur cholim*, a sub-set of the overall
mitzvah of loving one's fellow). *Bikkur cholim* consists of the following aspects:
1. taking care of the sick person's physical needs; 2. improving his mood; and
3. praying for his recovery. (See Ramban, *Toras HaAdam, Sha'ar Michush; She'elos
u'Teshuvos Tzitz Eliezer*, vol. 5; *Ramat Rachel*, ch. 3).

Communicating Complex Ideas

Because conflict naturally arises due to miscommunication, whether you're speaking to an individual or to a group, there are five rules that will help you explain complex ideas and ensure that the information is effectively conveyed.

Five Rules

1 **Focus.** Don't introduce too many new ideas or concepts at one time. Hone in on a couple of key points. If you overwhelm the person, he will begin to block out the information.[1]

2 **Calm.** Whenever possible, present the information in the most casual, relaxed setting, without diluting the importance of your message. The human brain learns

---

1. To whatever degree is practical, reinforce your message with visual aids. Our ability to grasp complex ideas is enhanced when we can put a picture to the words. Mind mapping is one such method in which ideas are given visual representation to increase comprehension and recall. A mind map is a diagram based on a central theme that is used to represent ideas, tasks, or other items linked to, and arranged in, a non-linear fashion. Mind maps are often used to aid in problem solving and decision making.

complicated ideas best when we are not anxious or otherwise preoccupied.[2]

3 Expectation.[3] Numerous studies demonstrate the powerful role that expectation plays in comprehension and execution, and include such findings as (a) girls who were told that they would perform poorly on a math test did so;[4] (b) assembly line workers who were told that the job was complex and difficult performed less efficiently at the same task than those who were told that it was easy and simple;[5] and (c) adults who were given fairly complex mazes solved them faster when told that they were based on a grade-school level.[6]

The implications of expectancy are significant for every area of daily life, whether you're dealing with children, employees, or the attendant at the gas station. Your expectation of a person's success will help to increase the individual's actual performance.[7]

---

2.   When we are nervous, we take things more literally, our minds try to get their bearings, and we often cannot see beyond face value. For instance, we will often have trouble processing sarcasm, because it requires a non-logical perspective, and this shift in thinking takes time.

3.   More on the power of expectation can be found in Chapter 25.

4.   J. R. Becker, "Differential Treatment of Females and Males in Mathematics Classes," *Journal for Research in Mathematics Education* 12 (1981), pp. 40–53.

5.   R. Rosenthal, *Experimenter Effects in Behavioral Research*, enlarged edition (NY: Irvington Publishers, Inc., 1976).

6.   L. Jussim and K. D. Harber, "Teacher Expectations and Self-Fulfilling Prophecies: Knowns and Unknowns, Resolved and Unresolved Controversies," *Personality and Social Psychology Review* 9:2 (2005), pp. 131–155.

7.   The well-known placebo effect can induce physiological changes such as lowering blood pressure or controlling cholesterol levels. With no more than a sugar pill, a patient's body may react as if it were given the actual medication. The expectancy effect is highly malleable and can be enhanced through a variety of factors. In one study, the response to a placebo increased from 44% to 62% when the doctor administered the sugar pill with warmth, attention, and

4 **Context.** When trying to communicate a complex idea, make sure that the person understands the entire picture. For instance, you can repeat the following sentence back and recall it later with great ease: "The four boys were learning Torah in the corner room." But how long might it take you to memorize the following ten random words: "bat, go, fly, how, to, starter, never, hot, tremendous, and hen"? The former sentence is easier to remember because you know how the words relate to one another.

Explaining details and specifics without first making sure that someone knows the context, is like putting a puzzle together without knowing what the picture is.

5 **Review.** Information must be reviewed periodically or it is routinely forgotten. End with a summary and then ask the person to repeat back, in his own words, the idea that you have just expressed.

A Fresh Start

"The Sages (*Yoma* 29a) tell us that it is more difficult to master an idea we are already familiar with than one that is new to us. This is because we feel we understand it and do not concentrate on it as much as we should. Therefore, the Sages advise us to view Torah concepts as if they were new. We should reflect on these ideas as if this were the first time we were hearing them."[8]

---

confidence. See D. A. Drossman, P. Goldman, and A. J. Lembo, "Components of Placebo Effect: Randomized Controlled Trial in Patients with Irritable Bowel Syndrome," *BMJ, vol.* 336 (2008), pp. 999-1003.

8. Rabbi Simchah Zissel Ziv Broida, *Chochmah u'Mussar*, p. 199.

CHAPTER

Help Someone Open Up
and Be More Expressive

H e doesn't share; he hardly even talks. At best, he grudgingly offers monosyllabic responses. Whether you're attempting to communicate with a non-expressive child, a colleague, or someone with whom you are acquainted socially, the following strategies can be helpful in opening up communication.

Initiate Dialogue

In the Torah we observe how Yosef demonstrates the value of initiating conversation in a difficult situation:[1] "Yosef came to them in the morning. He saw them and behold! They were aggrieved." He then asks, "Why do you appear downcast today?" Yosef makes the first step, and inquires as to their welfare in order to get them to open up. From this we learn the importance of encouraging discussion, rather than waiting for the person to talk to us.

---

1. *Bereishis* 40:6–8. The chief cupbearer and chief baker to Pharaoh had been thrown into prison and placed under Yosef's care. One night they both dreamt a disturbing dream, and Yosef could see they were upset.

Begin by raising a subject which you think will interest him. Give him your undivided attention, and show that you are listening by expressing curiosity and asking him questions. Beware that he will shut down if he feels you are not focusing on him or are bored by what he has to say.

By showing interest in his ideas, ideals, and beliefs, you create a stronger emotional bond. This, in turn, makes him feel closer to you, and that paves the way for upfront and unguarded conversations.

How to Handle Delicate Situations

In certain situations, a person may feel uncomfortable about revealing his thinking, possibly because he doesn't want to hurt your feelings. In order to overcome the awkwardness, if you ask his opinion on something, try not to press the issue, even if his answer seems to be disingenuous. Rather, indicate in your response that you agree and that there is room for improvement.

Real-Life Scenarios

Example I

You're not sure if your co-worker really likes your idea for a new marketing campaign, even though she says that she does.

Q   Do you like the concept for my new idea?
A   Sure. It's very original.
Q   Well, what would it take for you to love the idea?

Example II

You want to know if your son is looking forward to going to camp this summer.

Q Are you excited about camp next month?
A Yeah. It'll be fun.
Q What would it take for you to be really excited about going?

Example III

Q Do you like my new patio deck?
A Sure, it looks fine.
Q How do you think I can make it look even better?

No one likes to be put in a situation where they feel they have to defend themselves. As you can see, the people described in these scenarios feel comfortable answering honestly because your questions demonstrate to them that you are aware that everything's not perfect.[2] By seemingly asking a new question, you are essentially aiming to have your initial question answered, and will hopefully open up the discussion toward a meaningful dialogue.

---

2. Sometimes children—especially adolescents—are prone to moodiness, and even if they have positive feelings about an upcoming event, such as camp, they may not want to talk about it with their parents, or may not be in the mood to be enthusiastic. Also, in the case of someone who asks their colleague their opinion about an idea, most times a simple, "I like it," should be taken at face value. It could antagonize the person if it seems you are fishing for further praise, or trying to read his mind by suspecting that he isn't really happy with the idea. Therefore, you should apply this strategy only in instances where you believe that the person wants to be more forthcoming but is concerned that you might be uncomfortable with the full truth.

Gathering Specific Information

It can be frustrating to ask a question only to get a vague or apathetic response. The following approach is effective in eliciting more direct and honest answers. Notice how much more effective the "B" technique is than the traditional "A" technique.

A

Comment: "I don't think the sales meeting went very well."
Response: "How come?"
Comment: "I just don't, all right!"

B

Comment: "I don't think the meeting went very well."
Response #1: "How do you know when a prospect is interested?"
Response #2: "Did someone say something or was that your impression?"
Response #3: "Were you having an off day or were they just not qualified?"

If you ask for clarification, the person feels encouraged to respond. Asking a broad question in response to a general statement just provokes a general response.

A

Comment: "I don't know if I could."
Response: "What do you mean, you don't know? or Why can't you?"
Comment: "I just don't know, all right?"

B

Comment: "I don't know if I could."

Response #1: "What, specifically, prevents you?"

Response #2: "What would have to happen for you to be able to?"

Response #3: "What would have to change if you did?"

You'll notice in the above scenario that sometimes the person himself hasn't given the matter much thought. By asking these focused questions, you are giving him an opportunity to examine his own motives and thoughts, which, in turn, gives you a clearer answer.

11

The Gentlest Way to Break Unpleasant News

When you are in a situation where you have to be the bearer of bad news, you can considerably alter a person's reaction by adjusting the way you deliver the information.[1]

Language in Thought and Action

Language has a powerful impact on our perception of, and feelings toward, a situation. It is for this reason that good salespeople will not tell you to, "sign the contract," but will rather suggest that you, "okay the paperwork." Even though both phrases point to the same action, it has been ingrained in us that we should be wary of signing contracts without first having a lawyer review it. But okaying the paperwork, that's something you can do without worrying.

---

1. Unless there is a necessity, one should not be the bearer of bad news. Bad news makes a person sad, upsets his affairs, and disrupts his *avodas Hashem* (ability to properly serve God). This is what King Solomon refers to in *Mishlei* (10:18): "One who utters negative news is a fool." On the other hand it is a mitzvah to tell good news, since one makes the listener happy and invigorated. If one knows good news pertinent to the listener, one should hasten to tell him. (See *Sha'arei Tzedek—Hilchos Bein Adam l'Chavero* 1:17).

Politicians understand more than most people, the power of words to influence attitude and behavior. During a military action, we would rather hear of collateral damage than be told that civilian property was accidentally destroyed; and we are not as disturbed hearing of friendly fire as we would be to hear that our soldiers shot at our own forces. And, of course, when watching the morning news, we are less moved being told of "casualties" than we would be if the reporter used the word "deaths."

Because language is the basis of thought, and emotion is the extension of thought, you can influence a person's reaction to a situation by choosing the right words.

As a result, you want to avoid harsh language and words that have a strong negative connotation and produce an automatic visceral reaction. In much the same way that a body goes into shock if there is an overload of pain, the mind is similarly traumatized when confronted with jarring language.[2]

"God said to Avram, 'Go for yourself from your land, from your relatives, and from your father's house to the land that I will show you.' "[3] The Ramban notes that the Torah conveys Avram's test in ascending order of difficulty. This was done in order to mentally prepare him for his new mission. If he were to have heard the most challenging aspect of his mission first,

---

2. Neuroscientists have formulated an explanation in recent years for what happens in the brain during these word-induced emotional short-circuits. The amygdala, a small almond-shaped nucleus within the limbic system of the brain, selects and ties together the varied experiences that make up our lives. Because of the amygdala, some of the stimuli that bombard us every second are imbued with positive or negative emotions. They are then recorded in the brain, where they provide underpinnings for memory and personality (R. Restak, *The Brain Has a Mind of Its Own: Insights from a Practicing Neurologist* (NY: Crown Trade Paperbacks, 1991).

3. *Bereishis* 12:1.

he might have frozen in fear, and may not have deemed himself capable of undertaking it.[4]

Elsewhere the Torah states, "God tested Avraham . . . and He said, 'Please take your son, your only one, whom you love— Yitzchak—and go to the land of Moriah; bring him up there as an offering.' "[5]

God did not immediately reveal the identity of the sacrifice to Avraham. *Chazal*[6] record the dialogue between God and Avraham. God says, "Take your son." Avraham replies, "But I have two sons. Which one should I take?" "Your only one." "But each of them is the only one of his mother." "Whom you love," God answers. "But I love them both." "I mean Yitzchak," God finally responds.

The *Midrash* asks, "Why did God not immediately reveal the identity of the offering to Avraham?" The Sages explain that the gradual revealing of the identity of the sacrifice was designed foremost to avoid shocking Avraham lest he be accused of complying in a state of disoriented confusion.[7]

The Torah provides another lesson of how startling news— even when positive—should be relayed. After Yosef reveals his true identity to his brothers, they returned home, but they were afraid to tell their elderly father that Yosef was indeed alive, fearing the good news would prove to be too much of a shock. So they gave a harp to their young niece Serach, daughter of Asher, and told her to play and sing for her grandfather. She

---

4. *Moreh Nevuchim* 3:24.

5. *Bereishis* 22:1-2.

6. *Sanhedrin* 89b.

7. Rashi, commentary to *Bereishis* 22:2. The second reason stated was to make the commandment more precious to Avraham by arousing his curiosity, and to reward him for complying with each additional detail.

played the harp and sang that her uncle Yosef was still alive and was the viceroy of Egypt. This enabled Yaakov to absorb the news without harm.[8]

Memories

Language also alters our perception of how we remember things. Research by E. F. Loftus[9] into eyewitness testimony indicates that the way a question is phrased substantially impacts on how we recall the details. For instance, regarding a traffic accident, those who were asked how fast the car was going when it *collided* into another car gave higher estimates than those who were asked how fast the car was going when it *hit* the other car.

Breakthrough research on memory and feelings is currently being conducted. James McGaugh, a professor of neurobiology at the University of California, Irvine, has done research that indicates that our memories are highly malleable—they take time to form in our brains (and possibly never fully and completely solidify).[10] Therefore, while memory is still forming, it's possible to strengthen or weaken it. It all depends on the stress hormone adrenaline. When a person undergoes a traumatic event, he experiences intense fear and helplessness, which stimulate adrenaline. Days, months, or even years later, the memory remains excessively strong.

The drug Propranolol sits on the nerve cell and blocks the production of adrenaline; it is adrenaline that intensifies an

---

8.   *Midrash Sechel Tov, Bereishis* 45.

9.   E. F. Loftus, *Eyewitness Testimony* (Cambridge, MA: Harvard University Press, 1979).

10.   This study is being coordinated though the Veteran's Hospital at Ft. Miley, San Francisco.

experience and keeps it locked in one's memory in a heightened state. Consequently, even after-the-fact, people who received this adrenaline-blocking drug while thinking about a past trauma were able to form a new association to the event and in some instances, transform their feelings towards it. It becomes clear, then, that it is not the circumstance, but rather *our thoughts about the situation*—and the corresponding physiological effect—that give rise to our emotions, and determine its impact and lasting influence.

Adjusting Reality

When a person becomes upset about an event in his life, it's because of one or more of three cognitive beliefs: (1) he feels that the situation is permanent; (2) he feels that it is critical, meaning that it's more significant than it really is; and (3) he feels that it is all-consuming, that it will invade and pervade other areas of his life.

When any or all of these beliefs are present, our anxiety and despondency are increased. Conversely, when we think of a problem as temporary, isolated, and insignificant, it doesn't concern us at all. By adjusting one or more of these factors, you can instantly alter a person's attitude and make it more positive.

Another component, which should be part of your overall strategy, is based on the law of contrast. This law states that we don't think and see something as it is, in its own merit, but in relation to other things. In essence we contrast and compare. By contrasting the situation with something worse it's perceived more favorably.

For example, if you bring your car to the mechanic and he tells you that you need new brakes, you might be displeased.

If, however, he were to first tell you that you might need a new engine, a new transmission, and a new exhaust system, only to inform you an hour later that you just need front brakes, your thinking may be, "Whew, I got away lucky this time." It's not the information itself that is so crucial, but rather its context and how it relates to everything else.

Real-Life Scenarios

Although it depends entirely on the situation, this strategy will cushion the emotional impact of unpleasant news. In the following case, a physician determines that his patient has diabetes. Look at the difference in the two approaches below, and decide that if you were the patient, which doctor would you rather hear the news from?

Dr. A

Mr. Doe, I'm sorry to have to inform you, but you have diabetes. My laboratory tests confirmed this just now. And as you may or may not know it can be life-threatening and you can face severe complications like amputation and blindness. Everything in your life has got to be changed from this moment on—what you eat, how you exercise, and so on. I'm truly very sorry.

Dr. B

Okay, you're in good health except for a variance in your blood sugar levels. I'm pleased with these results and that you came in when you did because it could have turned into something much worse. You're in good company, too; there are millions of other folks who have diabetes; that's the technical name for it. And the best news is that it's completely controllable and when properly cared for, you won't even be aware of it. As a matter of fact, I think you've had this for quite some time and you'll see with an improved diet and exercise program you'll have a lot more energy and vitality.

Both doctors delivered the same information, but Doctor B gave the news in smaller increments which allowed his patient to begin to accept and internalize the new situation, significantly lessening the impact. He used softer language and conveyed that there were positive aspects to the situation such as improved overall health. His entire tone was encouraging and he used phrases such as "I'm pleased we caught this . . ." instead of "I'm sorry . . ." Of course the patient will need to be informed of other details, but in time. As is true in many areas in life, presentation is everything.[11]

---

11.   An example of the power of presentation can be found in Rashi on *Vayikra* 16:1, who cites a parable (from *Toras Kohanim*) of two doctors. The first doctor instructs the patient: "Do not eat cold food, do not lie in a damp, chilly place." The second doctor repeats the instruction, but adds " . . . so that you will not die like the other man." The additional words of the second doctor impacts more strongly; and in some cases this is necessary. However, when your objective is solely to communicate information, and not to influence behavior, the approach of the first doctor is preferred.

Conflict Resolution

No More Tug-of-War:
When You Both Want What's Best

D ifferences of opinion often emerge in situations involving preference, approach, and taste—where there may be no clear choice or objective truth. When each side wants to accomplish the same end, but disagree on the methods to achieve that goal, let us first reflect on the wise words of King Solomon, who reminds us that, "Two are better than one."[1] Often, we are so entrenched in our position that we fail to consider that the other person's approach may not be so bad after all—and in fact, may be better than our own.

It is natural for two people to have differences of opinion. The situation only becomes contentious when the two parties do not respect each other. If we stubbornly insist on having our way, we may have won this particular battle, but the next time a dispute arises, there will be even greater contention. It is essential then, to address the true source of the tension in addition to the details of the dispute. The moment mutual respect has been achieved, many of our differences often fade into insignificance.

---

1. *Koheles* 4:9.

The reality is that we care very little about socks being left on the floor, what color to paint the walls, or where to eat. We really are arguing over the right to be heard and the desire to have our feelings validated.[2]

In an intriguing study,[3] a group of researchers asked hundreds of felons—convicted of crimes ranging from drug possession and fraud to armed robbery—to participate in a survey about how fairly they felt they had been treated during the legal process.

Regardless of the severity of their crime, or the sentence received, respondents weighed most heavily one single factor: how much time their lawyers spent with them. The more time given to them, the more satisfied they were; if they were neglected—and so felt disrespected—by their lawyers, even when given a light sentence, they reported less satisfaction with the legal process.

Human beings experience pleasure when they give to other people. So why are we slow to back down and let the other person have their say? A person holds back from another because he does not feel that his own emotional needs are being met. Therefore, if the person with whom we are arguing knows that we hold him in high esteem, he won't feel the need to assert himself in other, more confrontational, ways.

When we find ourselves in ongoing disputes over minor issues, use the techniques in Chapter 2 as a preventative measure, as well as the following strategies for specific situations.

---

2.   "When someone feels inner hatred towards another person, even a minor offense can arouse feelings of animosity. Even though what has actually occurred right now could be trivial, the previous negative feelings create quarrels. But when someone feels love for another person, he is able to forgive whatever the other person does." (The Vilna Gaon on *Mishlei* 10:12).

3.   J. T. Casper and B. Fisher, "Procedural Justice in Felony Cases," *Law and Society Review* 22 (1998), pp.483-507.

1. Reciprocal Persuasion: You Scratch My Back, I'll Scratch Yours

Psychologist Robert Cialdini introduced a principle in psychology called reciprocal persuasion, which basically states that if you change your mind about something because I ask you to, then when you ask me to change my mind about something, I'm more likely to do it.

Wherever truthful, if you let a person know that you have rethought your position because of something that he has suggested, he will be more likely to change his mind because of you in the future. In addition to invoking the law of reciprocal persuasion, you are also demonstrating that you have confidence in his judgment and value his input.

2. Adopt a Two-Sided Argument

Studies reveal that when a person holds an opposing view to that of your own, you should adopt a two-sided argument.[4] If you ignore his point of view, he will believe you to be unreasonable. Therefore, present a balanced approach by laying down both sides of the issue.

3. Do Me a Favor

When it is clear that each of you believe that your position is the correct one, simply *ask* him to acquiesce on this issue as a *favor.* Tell him that:

---

4.   B. H. Kniveton, "Negotiation Training and Social Psychology," *Industrial Relations Journal,* vol. 4 (1975), pp. 59–72.

1 You thought about his position—what he wants, does, likes, and so on—and realize how he feels about it.

2 You know that he doesn't agree with you and that he feels he is right, but you would still like him to go along with your way of thinking.

3 You will do it his way, without hesitation or conversation, if it becomes clear that your way isn't working. And if it's a one-time only situation, then agree to do something else his way if your approach is not effectual.

Now he's doing something *nice*—a favor for you. The psychological dynamics change, because he can acquiesce while still being right, and without having to adjust his thinking.

By trying to get him to do what you want, you have two obstacles: the ego and the intellect. With the approach suggested above, you avoid engaging his ego; you are not telling him he is wrong, and so he does not have to defend his position.

Instead of feeling like he's *giving in* (which is tantamount to an act of weakness), he feels empowered because he is *giving to you*. It is the difference between giving a donation and being mugged. In both cases, money is moving from him to another person; one instance is empowering, while the other is emotionally draining.

In fact, there is another psychological force in play. This technique moves the others' perception from an economic model to a social model. In *Predictably Irrational*, the author recounts that when the AARP asked some lawyers to offer a range of simple and inexpensive services to needy retirees for $30 an hour, they overwhelmingly refused. The request was then changed, but instead of offering a higher fee, the lawyers were asked to offer the same services for *free*. The result? *Nearly all of them agreed.*[5] When presented with the initial offer of $30 the lawyers made an economic decision and concluded that it was not worth it. However, when the fee was removed altogether, it moved the decision into the social realm and away from the ego-entangled economic model. No longer was it a question of, "Does this make sense?" but rather, "Is this the right thing to do?"

Just Because

A study done by Langer, et al., found that the word *because* holds an astonishing power. Asking to cut in front of people using the copying machine, the researcher said, "Excuse me, may I use the Xerox machine?" to which a little over half of the people agreed. The fascinating thing is that Langer found she could get almost everyone to comply when they changed the phrasing of the request to: "Excuse me, may I use the Xerox machine because I have to make copies?" The reason was nonsensical. Of course you need a copying machine in order to make copies. So why does it work so effectively? Because the word "because" triggers an unconscious expectation that a valid reason will follow. We hear something and we have an almost reflexive response to accept it. Whether the sentence makes sense or not, we assume it does and, therefore, we don't bother to process the explanation.[6]

---

5.   R. H. Thaler and C. R. Sunstein, *Nudge: Improving Decisions About Health, Wealth, and Happiness* (Yale University Press, 2008).

6.   E. Langer, A. Blank, and B. Chanowitz, "The Mindlessness of Ostensibly Thoughtful Action: The Role of 'Placebo' Information in Interpersonal Interaction," *Journal of Personality and Social Psychology* 36 (1978) pp.635–642.

Real-Life Scenarios

We'll use a generic script here, so plug in the situation that is relevant to you: an argument with a spouse, boss, friend, neighbor, etc.

> "Binny, I'd like to get your thoughts on a small investment opportunity."

A few days later or whenever appropriate, bring a small gift; and when truthful, let the person know that things worked out well. "I just want you to know that I took your advice, and you were right about it, and it worked out great. I really appreciate your taking the time to help me with it. I told Andy all about it, too."

Should you happen to see or speak with him afterward, remember to thank him again.

> "I was going to go an entirely different way, but I'm glad you talked to me about doing it the other way. You could not have been more right."
>
> [Then, when he's in a fairly good mood] "By the way, (regarding which hotel to stay in/the best mover to use/ what investment to make) I know that you believe your way is less expensive/more proven/better in the long run, but do you think it's possible for us to try out my idea? I'd really like for us to try it this way. It would mean a lot to me."

Often we are so consumed with making our point and winning the argument that we lose sight of what we really want: having the other person acquiesce.

Additionally, such a strategy is useful, since if he wants what is best, he will get to do it his way should your way not work. And most importantly, we deal with the other person in a respectful and considerate manner, thus avoiding conflict and hurt feelings.

CHAPTER

13

Simple Methods for Fair
and Equitable Division

Whether you're dividing up toys between children or dis-
tributing the assets of an estate, the following strategies
can be used to resolve conflict while minimizing resentment.

Solution 1: You Divide, I Pick

One party divides the items into two groups, and the other
party selects one of the piles. This is one of the oldest and most
equitable ways to distribute or divide anything. It provides a
checks-and-balances situation whereby each side is able to
assert its demands.

Now, if both parties want the same *item*, each person should
place into a virtual pile those items he is willing to give up in
order to gain this one item. After that is done, the technique is
the same—one person divides and the other picks.

Solution 2: Casting Lots

Sortition is the technical term for casting lots. It is an equal-
chance method of selection, like a lottery, where each person

has the same odds. The Vilna Gaon writes, "In certain situations people can resolve their practical disagreements about the course of action to take by casting lots. Rather than trying to overpower each other, they can settle their quarrel in this peaceful manner."[1]

Solution 3: You, Me, Me, You

Another universally practiced method is to alternate choosing, with one person going first, then the second party having two picks. It then alternates again evenly, with one pick per party, back and forth, until all the items have been selected.

Real-Life Scenarios

SCENARIO A: Two workers are arguing over who gets the bigger office.

Solution 1: Since there's only one office, other items such as a parking space, a nicer chair, and an oak desk, are thrown into the mix. One person divides everything into what he believes are two equal piles. The other person is then asked to pick whichever collection he wants. It is possible that he may forgo the group with the office, opting instead to have some of the other items. The one who divided the piles may get the office in exchange for what he considers to be an evenhanded trade: the items in the pile that the other person chose.

SCENARIO B: Two children are arguing over toys that were given to them both to share for Chanukah.

---

1. The Vilna Gaon in his commentary on *Mishlei* 18:18.

Solution 2: All the toys are either listed or placed in front of each child. They alternate in picking a toy to be placed in their pile, until all of the toys are chosen (or broken).

Solution 3: An offshoot of the previous solution, here, the child picking first selects one toy, while the child picking second is able to choose two toys. This strategy can be more effective when both parties insist on being the first to select, or where the items are of disproportionate value.

We should not lose sight that the issue of whether one feels entitled is irrelevant regarding one's obligation to fulfill the laws of the Torah. A person must not simply aim to always get his way, rather he should ask himself in all situations what his responsibility is, regardless of his personal gain.

14

The Family Feud over Money: End It Now

Money is the single biggest cause of family rifts. Although arguments over money are often based on legitimate claims, where the money is genuinely needed by one of the parties, there are also many cases where people sever relationships with each other over money they don't even need. Siblings battle it out in court for millions of dollars from their parents' inheritance. The winner gets to move the money to an account with his number. Never seen, never touched, never used.[1]

There are generally two main types of conflicts involving money:

Type A: Arguments over Spending

This is where family members fight over who spends how much and on what. Every time one person comes home with some-

---

1. A qualified Rabbi should be consulted regarding the writing of a will and its disbursement, as there are many halachic details that need to be taken into account, including the firstborn brother's right to a double portion of the inheritance. See *Shulchan Aruch* (*Choshen Mishpat* 276–289), regarding the laws of inheritance.

thing new, it's an argument waiting to happen. For example, the wife thinks her husband is a spendthrift, while the husband thinks his wife is stingy.

Solution

Establish a budget (or call it a *spending strategy*, if the word budget is offensive or loaded). Rather than having to answer to someone, a budget allows a person who is spending the money to feel a sense of independence; instead of arguing over each purchase, the couple needs to discuss only periodically the scope of their budget.

But wait a minute! Lots of families have budgets. And if you've lived in an apartment with thin walls, you know that some of these people *still* argue. Loudly. This is true because unless two rules are established and adhered to, a budget cannot work.

Rule 1: The person giving the money must pass no judgments and make no comments on *how* the money is spent. No looks, no faces, no sarcasm. Nothing.

Rule 2: The person spending the money must be considerate and sensitive when it comes to purchasing items that he believes will cause the other to be annoyed.

Type B: Allocation of Funds

There is a fixed sum of money, with more than one person laying claim to it. Whether it's Uncle Ephraim's estate or an argument over who should pay for the broken fence, money seems to bring out the worst in people.

Phase 1: Build Up the Bond

It helps to spend time together, without talking about the matter at hand. If you can agree to put this issue to the back burner and focus on the relationship itself, either the money problem will resolve itself, or your relationship will be in a better shape to withstand the ensuing conflict.[2]

Rabbi Eliyahu Dessler writes: "When each person tugs in the opposite direction, there will be conflict. Since they are not focusing on their common goals they will constantly quarrel. When people focus instead on their common goals, the differences between them no longer cause strife, and their relationship will be peaceful."[3]

It's not that refocusing our attention instantly neutralizes the differences, but rather the overall relationship improves when people spend time working on shared goals, beliefs, values, and objectives rather than being at odds; and the stronger the relationship, the more easily disagreements can be resolved.

When you do eventually get together to talk about the issues, choose a laid-back and peaceful setting. Studies show us that anger, a significant component of conflict, is reduced when we are in a non-threatening environment. A conversation at the zoo, for instance, is less likely to provoke animosity than having the conversation around a conference table in a lawyer's office.

---

2. Conflict over money is like a psychological illness in a relationship. And as with a physical illness, there are two complementary strategies for healing it successfully. A malignant tumor, for instance, is treated directly by attacking it using chemotherapy or radiation therapy. Unfortunately, this weakens the person's overall immune system. A second method used in conjunction with traditional treatment, though not often used enough, is to boost the immune system. Doing so gives the person the best statistical edge for survival.

3. Rabbi Eliyahu Dessler, *Kuntres HaChessed.*

At this point, you have two choices. Either seek a mutually agreed-upon resolution, or move on to Phase 2, if you feel the situation will have a better outcome by switching tactics.

Phase 2: Relinquish Control

Sincerely convey to the person that you believe him to be an honorable person; and tell him that you will leave the decision up to him and you will abide by it. He wants to get the best deal out of the negotiation. "I won," is what he wants to think afterward. But when we're in charge of a situation, we are more inclined to do what is fair to all sides because there is no ego-satiating gain in getting more.

The idea of giving someone control is well illustrated in the following story: A good friend of mine is the head fundraiser for a large nonprofit organization. Each day he asks people for hundreds of thousands, sometimes millions, of dollars. Occasionally, he will go back to the same donor—someone who just gave money a mere month ago—and ask for another donation. While some people think that this is an unusual practice, he continually develops great relationships with these donors. What is his secret to avoid offending them?

Simple. He doesn't ask for another donation. Instead *he asks if he can ask* for a donation. Do you see the difference in the dynamics? If he were to ask for money outright, he would put the other person on the defensive and risk coming across as ungrateful, thus creating a power struggle. But by *asking if he can ask*, he puts the donor in control, and, as such, eliminates his defenses. Why? Because the donor can simply say no to the question, and not have to say no to the request for money.

Another application of this psychology was used by a very savvy woman while speaking to a large crowd on a controversial subject. Her colleague, during his presentation, had been subjected to yelling, screaming, and booing from the crowd. He walked off the stage in the middle of his talk. Now it was her turn to face the mob. She walked to the podium and said the following: "You were all very rude to Joseph, and that made him angry. If you are like that to me, you are going to make me cry." She got a smattering of laughter from that line and then spoke for nearly forty minutes, *uninterrupted.*

She managed to completely disarm the audience. What's going on in the mind of the listeners? What would there be to gain by making a grown woman cry? Nothing. They had won the power struggle. Yes, they could make her cry if they wanted to. Okay. Let's hear what she has to say. We still have power over her. She told us that much herself.

Phase 3: A Shift in Perspective

As a third party—or with the help of one—help each side to see the situation from the other person's point of view. In a situation such as this, we usually see things only from our limited perspective and rarely seek to expand beyond our desires. That's what being self-centered is—the experience that you are at the center of the universe. When we have a greater appreciation of the other person's needs, it makes it easier for us to want to accommodate them.

Phase 4: When All Else Fails . . .

If you cannot agree on who gets the money, perhaps you can agree to donate it to charity or to a cause. In that way, not only do both parties find common ground, but they are helping a third party.

One Great Solution

The *Shulchan Aruch* (*Choshen Mishpat* 12:2) strongly encourages the parties to make concessions among themselves in order to reach a compromise. If they are unable to do so, they can select an independent party to represent their respective interests, and these chosen parties will then meet and attempt to work out a compromise. A spin-off on this idea is to write down all the details of the dispute that both parties agree are the facts. Give the list to one person who is not overly familiar with what is going on. Let him read it and decide. This is an objective way to conduct your own mini-trial. If each person truly believes he is right, then he will feel comfortable turning to a neutral party. People are only reluctant to agree to such a suggestion if they fear that what is reasonable would be less than what they are hoping for.

If the phases cannot be implemented because there is no contact or communication between the two sides, you don't have a relationship conflict. You have a money conflict. If money is the objective and not the relationship, the conflict will not be solved without a fight. If money is more important, then *that* becomes the objective. It is a matter of values. What does each person want more?

Real-Life Scenarios

Two brothers are fighting over who gets the money from the sale of their deceased grandmother's house. Zev thinks he's entitled to the money because he took care of her when she was ill and paid most of her expenses. Shimon thinks he's entitled to it because, unlike Zev, he really needs the money and would have helped more if he hadn't been working two jobs to make ends meet.

They both agree, with the help of a third party, to put the issue of money to the side for now, and just spend time together talking and doing things unrelated to the situation.

As they begin to strengthen their relationship, Shimon, who now recognizes that his relationship with his brother is more important than money, approaches Zev in order to make peace.

The third party shows each brother how he can see the situation from the other's perspective and makes them aware of issues they might have overlooked.

> "Zev thinks he deserves the money because he spent more than twice that on her medication and nurses."
>
> "Shimon is looking to turn things around and wants the money to start a small business. He wants to be able to stand on his own two feet like his big brother, and he sees this as his chance."
>
> Shimon to Zev: "You know what, our relationship means more to me than the money. I will leave it up to you to decide what you want to do."

Shimon does not then allude to the fact that he is concerned. He continues to treat his brother with respect and love. He finds that his brother, without a battle to fight, becomes more even-handed.

The dual themes of control and respect are most pronounced when it comes to money—because it is money which feeds our ego with a false sense of power. Only when the relationship is stronger can the issue of money be addressed and hopefully resolved. If you focus on the money, to the exclusion of all else, the relationship will eventually crumble.

PART 3

Paving a Path to Forgiveness

What to Do When You Say the Wrong Thing

We all say things we shouldn't. What is important is how we deal with the gaffe. If a slip-of-the-tongue at a family gathering, office meeting, or social setting causes you to inadvertently embarrass or offend someone, try the following strategy to smooth things over as quickly as possible.

Phase 1: Depersonalize the Impact

It's true that time is the great healer, but time can occassionally reinforce ill feelings. If your words get twisted, or you find yourself unintentionally offending someone, it is important to dilute the impact as soon as you can.[1] Otherwise your words may fester, and the offended party will grow more incensed.

This can be achieved by generalizing your comment, rather than making it just about that person. For example, if you

---

1. If the offended party was not present at the time of the derogatory comment (*lashon hara*), and the damage inflicted by the *lashon hara* can be repaired by persuading those who heard it not to believe the negative information, then one is not required to ask forgiveness (*Chafetz Chaim, Hilchos Lashon Hara, Be'er Mayim Chaim* 4:48).

inadvertently told someone you don't like their proposal on a work-related issue, qualify your original comment by adding that this is an idea you have heard other people adopt in the past, and that it has never resonated with you.[2]

"You know you're the third person to tell me that in the past few weeks. I hear what you're saying, but I just don't see it." By letting him know that other people have made the same recommendation, it dilutes the rejection of his idea, as it is not technically his idea—others have said the same thing and you dismissed it from them as well.

Phase 2: Apologize and Take the Blame[3]

Apologize and accept responsibility for your words, but do not do so immediately after your hurtful comment. If you apologize first, without first depersonalizing the impact, you are communicating that you are sorry for *saying* what you did, but you are

---

2.   If you say something completely inappropriate, do not try to defend your behavior or qualify your statement. Instead, respond with: "I feel so foolish." Those four words accomplish three critical objectives. First, it shows that you know what you did was unacceptable—which means that you're unlikely to do it again. Second, it shows that you're human and people actually like us more when we acknowledge something embarrassing and then take personal responsibility for it. Third, it shows complete honesty—and we are much more forgiving of an honest person. One who has complete remorse tears himself down, so there is nothing left for anyone else to do, except to build him back up.

3.   A person who has committed an interpersonal wrong (*bein adam l'chavero*)— in this case hurting someone with one's words—must meet a fourth condition crucial to the *teshuvah* (literally, "return") process: he must ask the offended party for forgiveness (*Yoma* 85b; Rambam, *Hilchos Teshuvah* 2:9; *Shulchan Aruch, Orach Chaim* 606:1). The first three stages of *teshuvah* are: 1. regret the wrong (*charatah*); 2. verbally confess the errant behavior before God (*vidui*), and 3. resolve to no longer engage in such behavior (*kabbalah le'asid*). (Rambam, *Hilchos Teshuvah* 2:2–3). These stages are discussed in greater detail in the following chapter.

not conveying that you did not mean what you said. When you make your apology after your disclaimer, it is generally received in a better light.

Phase 3: A Casual Follow-Up

If, after qualifying your statement and apologizing, you still believe there are lingering ill feelings, speak to the person in private about how you lost your temper. Once again, accept responsibility for your outburst.

Real-Life Scenarios

A boss tells his assistant that he is completely incompetent in front of a room full of people.

> Boss: "Sam, you messed up that account incredibly. How careless could you be?" [The boss, realizing that he spoke too harshly, then says] "Everyone is making too many mistakes around here and messing up left and right."
> [Pause] "You know what, everyone? I'm sorry, I'm just not myself today. I'm really annoyed about something else, not all of you. This is the third time I lost my temper today."
> [Later that day] "You know, Sam, I think I need a vacation. I've been so edgy lately."

In the above scenario, the boss has succeeded in diluting the full impact of his harsh words directed at Sam, and by apologizing publicly, demonstrates to everyone in the room that he regrets his choice of words.

How to Reestablish Important and Meaningful Relationships

W hen one person has clearly violated the respect, trust, and rights of another, the path to forgiveness lies in *restoring balance* to the relationship—be it personal or professional. It is in balance that we find justice, and in justice that we find forgiveness.

Phase 1: The Power of Repentance

So crucial to our emotional wellbeing is this process of repentance that our Sages tell us that before God created the world, He created the power of *teshuvah* (repentance).[1]

The Four Stages of Teshuvah:[2]

1 *Feel remorseful.* Genuine regret for our wrong actions is the first step towards releasing our guilt. We must be

---

1. "Great is *teshuvah*, that it preceded the creation of the world" (*Midrash Tehillim* 90:12).

2. Rambam, *Hilchos Teshuvah* 1:1.

genuinely ashamed of our actions, or we cannot truly be sorry for them.

2 *Stop the behavior.* If it was a one-time action, then there is nothing more to stop. However, if we are still engaging in the wrongful behavior, then we must stop it, and resolve in our hearts never to commit the sin again. If we cannot change immediately, we should devise a plan to gradually cease this behavior over a period of time, and stick to it. We should also create deterrents for ourselves in order to avoid repeating the same transgression. In this way, we make a statement to ourselves and others that we have changed and that we are taking action to ensure that our improved selves thrive.

3 *Confess before God.* By confessing before God, we offer aloud the commitments and sentiments that reside in our heart. We should say, "I have sinned with this behavior, I deeply regret my actions, and I declare before God, Who knows my innermost thoughts, that I will never do this sin again."

4 *Ask for forgiveness.* If we wronged an individual, then we must first ask forgiveness from that person before asking forgiveness from God.[3] (We'll delve more into this in Phase 4). We are not responsible for the other person's response, but we have to ask.

Phase 2: Humility and Respect

Before attempting to gain forgiveness, you have to move forward with the utmost delicacy.

---

3.   *Yoma* 85b; Rambam, *Hilchos Teshuvah* 2:9; *Shulchan Aruch, Orach Chaim* 606:1.

Be Humble. If you come into the situation with anything other than *complete humility*, you will not receive forgiveness. What does this mean? Negate your ego. *It's not about you*, it's about the other person.

A great *Mussar* leader, Rabbi Chaim Zaitchyk, writes: "There is a very powerful tool that will enable you to overcome many potential quarrels . . . by being willing to forgo illusionary honor and speaking to someone from a humble position."[4]

Due to Avraham Avinu's great humility, his ego did not enter into conversations; he was able to focus on making others feel good and honoring them by referring to himself as, "Your servant," and others as, "My master."[5]

The Torah provides another example of the might of humility. When Yaakov meets up with his brother Eisav after having fled for his life more than thirty years earlier, the Torah relates the following conversation:

"But Yaakov said, 'No, I beg of you! If I have found favor in your eyes, then accept my tribute from me, inasmuch as I have seen your face, which is like seeing the face of a Divine angel, and you were appeased to me.'"[6]

Humbling ourselves automatically deflates the other person's ego. Additionally, Yaakov insists that Eisav keep the gifts in spite of the fact that Eisav clearly says that he does not wish to accept them—prompting the soon-to-be discussed law of reciprocity.

---

4.   Rabbi Chaim Zaitchyk, *Ma'ayanei HaChaim*, vol. 3.

5.   *Bereishis* 18:3.

6.   *Bereishis* 33:10. According to the *Midrash* (*Bereishis Rabbah* 75:11), God was opposed to Yaakov for humbling himself exceedingly before Eisav by calling him *adoni* (my master) a total of eight times.

Show Respect. When you address the person and employ these strategies maintain the highest degree of respect. This means that you should not argue and scream your point, or show up at his office demanding that he listen to your side of the story. Rather, you should ask permission before you speak to him and perhaps even *prior* to initiating contact, if the relationship is severely strained. Approaching the situation with extreme deference, and even reverence, is a requisite for the process.

Ask for permission before you do anything. Leave right away if he does not want to talk to you and try again another time. (And if you're there only to be yelled at, that's fine, too.)

In our anger we often do the opposite of this and say such things as, "I drove all the way here you darn well better talk to me. I said I was sorry! What more do you want?" This adds fuel to the flames, as we further demonstrate a lack of respect. You *almost* don't have to say anything as long as the other person sees that you are doing everything possible within your ability to make things right again.

In a situation where the person will not even talk to you or there has not been any contact for some time, you may need to jump-start the relationship and put in a great deal of effort, such as flying to where the person is, dropping off a letter of apology, and then leaving without speaking to the person.[7] If you can make an investment—emotionally, financially, or any other way—and show genuine effort, even without immediate success, you help to gain traction.

---

7. One is required not only to exert himself physically but also to spend his own money to pursue peace. (Cf. *Mishnah Berurah* 656:8.)

Phase 3: Be Accountable

It is important for you to take full and complete responsibility for your actions. Do not shift blame or make excuses—this will only exacerbate the situation. Do not say something such as, "I got so upset because you did . . .", or, "I didn't think it was a big deal to . . . " Don't blame him for anything—his actions or yours—and don't minimize your role.

Phase 4: Sincerely Apologize

The Vilna Gaon states, "When the person you have wronged sees that you sincerely regret having hurt him and you will not repeat your error, he will forgive you. When your regret is sincere, you will find the proper words to say."[8]

Sometimes we forget to actually say the words, "I'm sorry." While these words alone are often not enough, they are necessary to your gaining forgiveness. Make sure that your sincerity comes across. Any apology that is not sincere will not be believed. And if you are not believed, then you will not be forgiven. If you are not truly sorry, then you will repeat your actions and put this person through more pain. If you're not truly sorry and remorseful, it might be time to reevaluate the relationship and yourself.

Moreover, in order for an apology to truly be effective, you must acknowledge that your actions hurt the other person.[9] Statements such as, "I am sorry, I know I hurt you, and caused

---

8. The Vilna Gaon's commentary on *Mishlei* 10:32.

9. One should specify the wrong (*Hilchos Teshuvah* 2:5, *Kesef Mishnah*, ad loc.), unless it is likely that it would embarrass the other person (*Magen Avraham* 606:0). (Quoted from Aryeh Kaplan, *The Handbook of Jewish Thought*, vol. 2 (Brooklyn, NY: Moznaim Publishing Corp., 1979), 17:46).

you pain. For that, I have nothing but regrets," convey thought-fulness and a desire to change.

Phase 5: Establish Peace of Mind

You have to answer the question, Why? Every wrong action comes down to the *same motivation*: fear. Not surprisingly, fear is the henchman of the ego. If you look closely at your actions, you will find fear at their root.

For example, stealing money because you like nice things is a surface explanation; stealing because you need to build up a frail self-image lies at the core of the behavior.[10]

Now your action is seen less as a betrayal that violated trust, and more as what it truly was—an irrational act of fear. Exposing your insecurities increases your vulnerability; this is in stark contrast to braggadocio and self-centeredness, an attitude you do not want to present.

If you are perceived as the one in control, he will resist further. That is why in relationships you rarely find both people jealous of each other. Only one can be; and the other routinely moves to a more neutral psychological position to strike a balance.

After explaining the root fear-based motivation, reestablish-ing your commitment to the other person and to the relation-ship is required. This includes a phrase such as, "You know that our friendship means everything to me and I care more about

---

10.   Let's illustrate this idea with a brief look at the phenomenon of a mid-life crisis. A person goes out and does all those things that he fears he's missed out on or thinks he will miss out on. He buys a sports car. Fear. He asks, "What hap-pened to my dreams, my youth? I'm scared." Why doesn't a person commit to marriage? Fear. "What if someone better comes along? What if it's a mistake?" It all comes back to fear. Fear is what makes us vulnerable and this is what you need to explore, to understand yourself. Then you need to relate that fear to the person you've hurt.

you today than I ever did" (if one wronged a friend). Or, "This job has always been the focus of my life; I planned on working here until I retired" (if one stole from his job).

Phase 6: Be Willing to Accept—and Even Offer— Consequences

An important phase in this process is to let him know that you are willing to face and accept any and all consequences of your actions. Your behavior demonstrated a lack of trust. Putting yourself in his hands and being answerable not just for your actions but for the aftermath, goes a long way toward establishing the power that he lost.

It is one thing to talk the talk, but things can fall apart if he thinks that you are trying to escape unscathed. In truth, your fate (at least with him) rests in his hands at this point. You can start by saying something such as, "I know what I did was wrong. You have every right to be angry with me. I'm willing to accept the full repercussions of my actions." You must begin to cede control with your words, or you may be further castigated as his way of setting things straight.

Phase 7: Solidify with a Specific Action

Actually making a change in your life will go a long way in letting him know that you are sincere. Actions shout while words whisper.

Explain to him how the set of circumstances that led to this event will never be repeated again. Part of his disturbance over your behavior is the unpredictability of your actions; that is, it's something that happened and could happen again without notice or warning. If you can assure him that you have disrupted the catalyst to your behavior you will help alleviate much of his anxiety.

Phase 8: Let Your Character Shine Through

Respect lies in identifying with the virtues of another person. On the other hand, when we choose to dislike someone, we associate him with his faults. The reasons we give for disliking him are his negative qualities: He is arrogant, annoying, and cheap. When we think of someone we like, we identify with his good qualities: He is kind, generous, and open-minded.

Does this mean that the person we like has no bad traits? Of course not—it's just what we *choose* to focus on. If we shift our attention, we can look at anyone in a different way.

He has lost respect for you and he's thinking that you may not be the person he thought you were. Pursue objectives that show your true character. He needs to respect you again as a person. It is hard to dislike someone whom we hold in high esteem. Let him see your true nature, so that your transgression is filtered through this favorable light.

Phase 9: Make Things Right

If you profited in some way, then you will have to give back more in order to set things straight—whether it be money or other items.[11] If you don't have what you wrongfully took, but

---

11.   In the case of physical theft or damage, one must make complete restitution as part of the *teshuvah* process (Rambam, *Hilchos Teshuvah* 2:9, *Hilchos Gezelah* 8:13). For *teshuvah* to be complete, one must cleanse himself of the taint of any illegal gain, even where restitution is not required by the law. Therefore he must make restitution for all profits and any other benefits he may have accumulated

can replace it, make every effort to do so as soon as possible. Let the person know your plan and progress. *And remember, it's important to continue on this path even if he is still not talking to you.*

Regardless of your relationship with the person, you are still obliged to do what is right and repay the debt. By continuing to do what is right despite not getting what you want—the relationship—you will begin to prove yourself to be the kind of person he wants back in his life.

Phase 10: Improving the Relationship

Ideally, you should demonstrate how the relationship will be better than it was before. The person you have hurt may be reluctant to return to the same damaged dynamic. No one wants to give up a lifeboat to go back to a sinking ship. But by showing him what happened and the consequent changes you've made to *strengthen* your commitment to the relationship, he is gaining something far stronger than what he lost.

Phase 11: Put Together a Specific and Painless Game-Plan

It's important to let the person know exactly how things can proceed: slowly, easily, and with him in control along every step of the way. Therefore, you want to *suggest* a game-plan that moves slowly but surely toward the objective of reestablishing

---

as a result of the act (*Sefer Chassidim* 599, 628). If there is a question as to the amount one should return, he should seek the advice of a Rabbi. Since one may be tempted to act to his own advantage, he should not rely on his own judgment (*Chayei Adam* 144:6; *Mishnah Berurah* 606:1, quoted in Kaplan, *The Handbook of Jewish Thought*, vol. 2, 17:40).

the relationship: ensuring that he has the option, at any time, to continue, stop, or change course.

Phase 12: A Mirror of Reality

If you are meeting with resistance, remember that the world is a reflection of you, and *you can only give away what you have—* whether it's love, fear, kindness or anger. If you want a loving person, you must be a person who loves. Kindness, for example, may exist in the world, but not in *your world*, if you yourself are not kind. The world is set up as a reflection, direct and pure. You cannot receive if you do not give.[12]

If you want to be forgiven, you may need to forgive others. If you are holding on to ill will over what someone has done to you, you cannot be authentic with the person you have injured. If you can resolve any anger you are holding on to—be it toward yourself or toward another person—you will find a smoother path ahead in resolving the current situation. In fact, our need to forgive others is the preparatory stage to *teshuvah;* and *teshuvah* is a necessary step towards others accepting us back into their lives.[13]

---

12.   The Talmud (*Yoma* 23a) states that when one overcomes his feelings of anger towards someone and acts magnanimously, he is forgiven for all his wrong-doings, since forgiving others at a time when one is angry is elevating, in that it's an expression of the soul ruling over the body.

13.   "When God favors the ways of a person, even his enemies will make peace with him" (*Mishlei* 16:7).

Give a Peace Offering

The Ralbag suggests that one should, "Prepare a special gift for the person who is angry at you. When he receives the gift, his anger will subside. We find an example of this in the Torah (*Bereishis* 43:11) when Yaakov told his sons to take the best possible gift to the man in authority in Egypt."[14] Indeed, some years earlier, in the Torah portion of *Vayishlach* we learn that Yaakov sent gifts to Eisav while simultaneously preparing for war against him, and we find that it did help to asuage Eisav's anger.

Real-Life Scenarios

Raphael gambled and lost money that his family could not afford to lose. His wife has recently learned of her husband's actions.

First, the husband listens to his wife, and does not raise his voice or interrupt when she is speaking or yelling. He approaches the situation with great humility, emotion, and respect. If he has not yet done *teshuvah*, he is sure to do it now.

> Raphael: "I was completely and utterly wrong. I am deeply, deeply sorry and I regret everything about it. I know what I did was wrong. You have every right to be angry with me. I'm willing to accept the consequences for my actions.

---

14.   Ralbag, ad loc.

"Even though I was drinking and don't remember much of what I did, I am fully responsible for putting myself in that situation and for what happened.

"I also want you to know that I've given up drinking completely, and I've already enrolled in a treatment program. I called our insurance to see about coverage for a therapist for me, or if you want, both of us can go, too."

Only if she asks specifically what happened should he proceed to give her the details—he should not bring this up unless she asks.

"I think maybe, if we are able to work things out, that without my drinking, we won't fight as much about other things. If we can move past this, I think things can be better than they ever were before.

"I don't know how I let this happen. I was scared, but I'm not sure why. (Here he elaborates on possible motivations.) But I love you and I am committed to doing whatever it takes to make things right and better than they were before.

"We can go at any pace you want. Then, after I'm in therapy for a bit, you can tell me what you want to do. (It's important for Raphael to end the discussion by putting his wife in charge of the situation.) Do you want me to leave now or may I stay? I will do whatever you ask me to."

Now Raphael has given his wife a sense of independence, power, and control over the relationship. The very things that were taken from her have been replaced, and he has put her in a psychological position in which she is more likely to be willing, able, and ready to give of herself emotionally, in the form of forgiveness and reconciliation.

Over the next few weeks and months, Raphael will prove himself as someone who is not only redeemable, but respectable as well. In addition, he should make himself as available as humanly possible to help demonstrate that he is willing to put whatever time, energy and effort is required into making the relationship work.

"I want you to know, too, that day or night, whenever, and whatever you need from me, I am going to be there for you. Is there anything that I can do for you right now?"

He then does it without question or hestitation to demonstrate his commitment and trustworthiness.

PART **4**

You Can Be
the Great Peacemaker

17

Help Anyone Gain Forgiveness: Strategies for Getting One Person to Simply Listen to the Other

B efore employing the techniques presented, you need to be satisfied and fully convinced that the person in the wrong has done *teshuvah*, changed his ways, and is truly remorseful. Most important, be sure that reconciliation is in the best interests of both parties.

When you are trying to encourage others, think first of how you can present your ideas so that they will be heard and understood. It is not sufficient to simply make your point.[1] The following tactics can be employed when attempting to reconcile two sides.

Rule 1: He's at the Controls

There is a reason why flight attendants will ask you to, "Take your seat," rather than instructing you to "Sit down." Asking

---

1 "Is it well with him?" (*Bereshis* 3:6). The Seforno comments that Yaakov's inquiry to Lavan's welfare, was so that he would know how best to approach him in conversation.

you to take your seat doesn't make you defensive, as the request puts you in charge—you are going to take your seat. Telling you to sit down puts the flight attendant in control. This subtle difference in the wording has a major impact on how we feel about the request.

Part of a person's reluctance to hear someone out is due to a feeling that once he commits to that, it will be harder for him to stop the process. As long as he keeps saying no, he is in control. But once he gives in to listening, he feels as if he loses some of his power. To combat this, you want to convey that he is in complete control. He can leave the conversation whenever he wants—he will not be begged to stay.

Also, give additional information before you ask him to again reconsider. Nobody wants to be thought of as wishy-washy, meaning that if he changes his mind without any new information he may be perceived, and think of himself, as inconsistent. Rather, before asking him to agree each time, offer some other bit of relevant data or remind him of something he may have forgotten. In this way he can make a new decision based on additional information instead of simply changing his mind.

Rule 2: A Calm State

Continuing with the above theme, disagreements and conflicts arise when two people are in *katnus d'mochin* or *constricted consciousness*, where each needs to take, rather than to give, in order to be emotionally nourished. It is impossible to have a productive conversation when two people feel out of control. For instance, arguments may easily ensue when people are worried about something. Why? Because they are dependent on the outcome of a situation about which they feel helpless.[2] Therefore, they are unable to communicate properly and give to each other; they are forced to take.

In an anxious or harried state, it becomes increasingly difficult for us to see beyond our own needs, and to look at the situation objectively and rationally. Similarly, a person who is in physical pain can have difficulty focusing on the needs of others. A migraine headache, for instance, produces a pain we cannot control, and so we may be more easily irked or angered when we find ourselves in such a situation.

The need for control explains why it is, while waiting in the doctor's office, we often feel magically better, because we know that relief (and control) is imminent. (The fact that your car stops making that funny noise when you bring it to the mechanic is an entirely different phenomenon well beyond the scope of this author's understanding.)

Be sure then, to speak to this person when he is relaxed and unhurried. If he is preoccupied with other matters, you will likely meet with great resistance.

Shake it Out

The sway of physiology on our emotions is startling. You can try this on yourself. Sit hunched over, legs drawn in, frown and put your head down. Stay that way for a few minutes. How do you feel? Chances are you feel pretty lousy. But now stand up, wave your arms, and shake your body. Notice how your entire emotional state changes.

---

2. Studies show that patients who are able to control their IV painkiller, dispense to themselves less of the drugs, and report feeling less pain. The sense of control alleviates the fear and anxiety that fuels the pain. See H. Chen, M. Yeh, and H. Yang, *International Journal of Medical Informatics* 74:6 (1996), pp. 437–445.

> By bending and moving our bodies, our minds in turn become more flexible toward other ideas and ways of thinking.

Rule 3: Harness the Power of Inertia

It is beneficial to observe how people process information. When it comes to doing something that we like, we do what's called *single-tasking*. When we think about things we don't want to do, we do what's called *grouping*. What does this all mean? Well, if you have to pay your bills but never feel like doing it, what is the thought process you might go through? You think, "I've got to get all of the bills together and organize them into different piles; get out my checkbook, stamps, and envelopes; address each letter; write out the check; balance the check-book . . ." and so on. When it comes to activities you enjoy, however, the steps are streamlined into clusters. For example, if you enjoy cooking, you think, "Go to the store and come home and make dinner."

If you dislike cooking, everything from waiting on line at the supermarket to cleaning the dishes afterward would enter into the equation. How can this be applied to our situation? If you want someone to agree to a meeting or reconciliation, you're going to emphasize to him that it will be *simple, quick,* and *easy*.

Sir Isaac Newton discovered that objects in motion tend to stay in motion, and objects at rest tend to stay at rest. He might as well have added that people in motion tend to stay in motion and people at rest tend to stay at rest. If you can get a person moving in the right direction, either physically or mentally, starting with something easy or perhaps fun, you will begin to generate positive momentum. [3]

Since the hardest thing to do is to begin,[4] consider the following: Research cited by behavioral economists found in one company, only twenty percent of employees had enrolled in a retirement plan after three months of employment. The form was then reformatted to make enrollment the *default* option, and participation shot above ninety percent.

Another study they conducted showed that placing fruit at eye level in school cafeterias enhances its popularity—and therefore desirability—by as much as 25 percent.

They write: ". . . harness the power of inertia. In a work setting, this could mean framing assignments so that the option perceived to be the path of least resistance is the one designed to get the bulk of the work done. For example, employees could be asked to either use a template to canvass a large group of people for their opinions on a given product, or compile the research and run a workshop, showing higher-ups why they should change their thinking about that product's launch. Most will likely opt for the structured—or templated—assignment, but the work gets properly done with a minimum of fuss."[5]

---

3.   The language that you use can also invoke the law of inertia. Seemingly innocuous words such as "as," "while," and "during" are such potent triggers that they are often used in hypnosis. For example, if you want cooporation, you're better off saying something such as, "While we're out, let's go by Jay's house, okay?" instead of, "When we go out, do you want to stop in and see Jay?" Do you see how easily the first sentence flows with the idea of seeing Jay? These words are influential because they are movement-oriented. Human beings think with words and these words—inherent in their definition—denote that two things are taking place simultaneously.

4.   Jewish tradition teaches that, "All beginnings are hard." (*Mechilta*, cited by Rashi on *Shemos* 19:5, regarding the acceptance of the Torah by the Jewish people).

5.   R. H. Thaler and C. R. Sunstein, *Nudge: Improving Decisions About Health, Wealth,*

Confirm Commitment

Angela Lipsitz and others report that ending blood-drive reminder calls with, "We'll count on seeing you then, okay?" and then pausing for response, increased the attendance rate from 62 to 81 percent. Just this one phrase increased the rate by about 20 percent.[6] When you initially make your request ask for a verbal confirmation to increase your chances of getting the person to follow through once he commits.

Rule 4: Internal Consistency

Studies in human behavior demonstrate that you can guide a person's thoughts by changing how he sees himself.[7] This allows you to change a person's self-perception so that it is flexible, giving and open-minded: the exact frame of mind necessary for achieving peace and establishing harmonious relationships.

Therefore, you might say something like, "I've always loved the fact that you aren't afraid to change your mind." Or, "You really know that communication is what a relationship is all about. I very much respect that." Or, "You never lose sight of what is really important in a relationship."

These comments make a person feel inspired to follow through, because as we leaned earlier, human beings have an

and Happiness (Yale University Press, 2008).

6. A. Lipsitz, K. Kallmeyer, M. Ferguson, and A. Abas, "Counting on Blood Donors: Increasing the Impact of Reminder Calls," *Journal of Applied Social Psychology* (1989), pp. 1057–1067.

7. G. Martin and J. Pear, *Behavior Modification: What It Is and How to Do It*, Eighth Edition (Prentice Hall, 2007).

inherent need to perform in a manner consistent with how they see themselves and with how they think others perceive them.

I remember once explaining this idea to a colleague. When he came into my office, I offered him some fruit. He hesitated for a moment and then gave an unsure, "No, thanks." I took a nice ripe apple and I saw that he was about to change his mind. That's when I said, "You know what I like about you? You're not wishy-washy. You make a decision and you stick to it. You're a man who knows what he wants." After I said that, it became very hard for him to ask for the fruit—as he later acknowledged—because it would shatter my image of him. Of course, I only let this go on for a minute before clueing him in, and then watched him eagerly devour a peach.

Another way to apply this psychology is to discuss *themes*, such as friendship, family, partnership, commitment to work, and a sense of decency—all qualities that most people aspire to identify with. "Isn't it amazing how some people don't know the definition of the word 'family'?" A statement such as this can be very powerful. In one sentence, you remind a person of his value system—what is important to him.

Rule 5: Motion Creates Emotion

A variation on the previous rule shows that when we take a small step in one direction, we are driven to maintain a sense of consistency by agreeing to larger requests.

Researchers asked homeowners if they would let them place a large "Drive Carefully" sign in their front yards. *Only 17 percent gave permission.* Other residents, however, were first approached with a smaller request. They were asked to put up a three-inch "Be a Safe Driver" window sign. Nearly all immediately agreed.

When approached a few weeks later, the homeowners were asked to place the gigantic sign on their front lawn. This same group overwhelmingly agreed—*76 percent consented*—to having the unsightly sign in their front yards.[8]

Simply, those who had agreed to the smaller request had reshaped their self-perception to include the definition that *they were serious about driver safety.* Therefore, agreeing to the larger request signified their continued commitment to the cause.[9]

Another study asked a group of people to call for a taxi if, while they were drinking, they became intoxicated. Half of them also signed a petition against drunk driving while the other half didn't. Those who did sign the petition were much more likely to follow through with calling the taxi service once they were impaired than those who did not sign the petition. As incredible as it sounds, a simple petition created such a strong unconscious drive that even though the subjects were inebriated, they stuck to their commitment.[10]

These findings lead to some astonishing conclusions. Since people have a strong need to be congruous with their self-concept,[11] when we vocalize, or in some way concretize, an opinion—*whether or not we believe it to be true*—we usually come to support it in time.

---

8.   J. L. Freedman, and S. C. Fraser, "Compliance without Pressure: The Foot-in-the-Door Technique," *Journal of Personality and Social Psychology* 4 (1966), pp.195–202.

9.   The *Mesilas Yesharim* describes this technique, "the external awakens the internal," with other details, at the end of Ch. 23.

10.   T. Taylor and S. Booth-Butterfield, "Getting a Foot in the Door with Drinking and Driving: A Field Study of Healthy Influence," *Communication Research Reports* 10 (1993), pp. 95–101.

11.   The *self-concept* is the way in which we perceive ourselves regarding our beliefs, personality traits, physical characteristics, and values.

Therefore, ask the person who was wronged to perhaps write a letter stating that he is open to hearing the other person (even if he plans on destroying it afterwards), or ask him to voice two reasons why a renewed relationship would be a good idea. Any action that gets him moving in the right direction helps to fuel his desire to make peace.

Rule 6: Leading by Example

Infomercials are a multi-billion dollar industry where each second is carefully scripted for the utmost impact. Legendary program writer Colleen Szot shattered a twenty-year sales record for a home-shopping channel with the change of just a few words. Instead of the familiar call to action of, "Operators are standing by, please call now," she rewrote the script to: "If operators are busy, please call again." The message implied, of course, is that others are calling in droves, so much so that you might not even be able to get through right away—this must be something good.

This principle is even more pronounced, not only when it comes to decision-making, but in doing what is right from a moral perspective. Knowing others "did the right thing" invokes an unconscious desire to do the same. It can even lead to an increase in blood donations, as researchers found after soliciting nearly 10,000 students at high schools. Students who viewed a slide show that mixed in thirty-eight photos of high school blood drive scenes were *17 percent* more likely to donate than those who did not see those pictures.[12] Simply viewing

---

12.   I. G. Sarason, B. R. Sarason, G. R. Pierce, E. N. Shearin, and M. H. Sayers, "A Social Learning Approach to Increasing Blood Donations," *Journal of Applied Social Psychology* 21 (1991), pp. 896–918.

photos of their peers donating blood prompted more students to do the same.

To incorporate this theme, introduce either in name, or in person, people who are known and respected by both parties, and who, when faced with a similar situation, rose above their nature, and made the choice to make peace.

Rule 7: A Matter of Obligation

If the person to whom you're speaking to is God–fearing, encourage him to consider these words from a great Sage, the Ralbag, who writes, "A person who sincerely fears the Almighty should forgive someone who wronged him when that person asks for forgiveness. He should do his best to return to the previous state of loving friendship that existed before the other person erred. We find in the Torah[13] that Yosef forgave his brothers for selling him into slavery as soon as they asked for forgiveness. He told them that because he feared God they need not worry. A person who fears the Almighty will not behave cruelly and will not refuse to grant forgiveness."[14]

It's About Peace

"Do things for the sake of the Creator and speak about them for their own sake" (*Nedarim* 62a).[15] We should seek to make peace because it is inherently right to do so, even without an apparent reason.

---

13. *Bereishis* 50:21.

14. *Ralbag*, ad loc.

15. Rashi s.v. *v'daber b'hen* reads the statement as: "Do things for the sake Heaven [i.e., the Creator] and speak about them for the sake of Heaven."

Rule 8: Risk Aversion

One of the chief missteps mediators make is to focus solely on the benefits—we go on at length about how good things will be once peace is achieved.[16] Your attempt to persuade however, will be more successful if you point out how resolving the conflict will also prevent negative consequences.[17]

The concept of framing information to influence a person's perception of the situation begins with an historic 1981 study by Tversky and Kahneman:

Imagine that the U.S. is preparing for an outbreak of an unusual Asian disease, which is expected to kill 600 people. Two alternative programs to combat the disease are proposed. Assume that the exact scientific estimates of the consequences of the programs are as follows:

- If program A is adopted, 200 people will be saved.
- If program B is adopted, there is a ⅓ probability that 600 people will be saved and ⅔ probability that no people will be saved.

---

16. Negatively framed outcomes shift in favor of your plan, even when it is riskier than another course of action. Called risky *choice framing effects*, human beings are more inclined to take a risk (e.g., elect a risky medical procedure) when potential outcomes are not positively framed (e.g., in terms of success rate) but rather framed negatively (e.g., in terms of failure rate). Simply put, we are more disposed to take a risk to avoid a loss than to achieve a gain. See Daniel Kahneman, and Amos Tversky, "Prospect Theory: An Analysis of Decision under Risk," *Econometrica* 47 (1979), pp. 263–291.

"There shall be seven years of famine" (*Bereshis* 41:27). The Ramban (ad loc.) comments that while Pharaoh's dream began with the good years, Yosef responded first to the bad years, in order to focus Pharaoh's attention to the potential disaster that could be avoided.

17. H. Leventhal, R. Singer, and S. Jones, "The Effects of Fear and Specificity of Recommendation upon Attitudes and Behavior," *Journal of Personality and Social Psychology* 2 (1965), pp.20–29.

Which program would you choose? When the programs were framed in this way, the researchers found that 72 percent of the respondents chose to save 200 lives rather than risk everyone's lives. However, they then posed the question to a second group of subjects with a twist and framed the alternatives differently.

- If program C is adopted, 400 people will die.
- If program D is adopted, there is a ⅓ probability that nobody will die, and ⅔ probability that 600 people will die.

In surprisingly stark contrast to programs A and B, 78 percent of the respondents chose D, the riskier alternative, when presented with programs C and D. If statistics is not your strong suit, choices A and C are exactly alike. Out of the 600 people, if "400 people will die," then "200 people will be saved." Likewise, choices B and D offer the same odds. If there is a "⅓ probability that 600 people will be saved," there is the same probability that—out of the 600—"nobody will die."

In the survival (or positive) frame, people are less likely to take risks to maintain survival. In the mortality (or negative) frame, risk taking is preferred more often to avoid death. Same information. Different presentation.

Rule 9: A Soul Story

Have you ever wondered why we enjoy hearing a moving story? Or for that matter, why it moves us at all? The reason is that such stories invariably bring out either a person's sense of altruism and purpose or vulnerability and fragility. In both cases, the ego is muted and the soul of the other resonates with ours. As we know, it is our ego that gives us the illusion of separateness. Hearing of a person who willingly discards his ego or has it stripped from him, instantly unites us. The barrier of "I am me and he is he," is broken down, and empathy emerges.

Before requesting a get-together invite him to listen to, watch, or read this type of story; it will help to place him in the right frame-of-mind, and to connect him to what is truly important.

Curiosity Factor

Human beings are driven by a need to satisfy their curiosity. From the celestial heavens to the missing sock in the dryer, we have an insatiable need to know *why*. Therefore, you want to let the resistant person know, that the reason for the other's actions is something that is extraordinary, if this is true, and that once he hears it, it will put the whole situation into proper perspective. Once you have his curiosity aroused, tell him the catch: the other person wants the chance to explain himself. He will also be moved to find out because he wants to learn that there were other circumstances, possibly beyond his control, that might explain the other's actions.

Real-Life Scenarios

A friend of yours, Yitzi, spoke *lashon hara* (evil speech or gossip) about his business partner, Danny, and Yitzi has come to you for help. Danny is furious because the slander has cost him a lot of business. He just wants to end the business arrangement and won't listen to anything Yitzi has to say.

First, meet with Danny privately and lay the groundwork by asking such questions as:

"Do you think forgiveness is important?" or, "How much of our happiness in life depends upon healing old wounds?"

Such querries will cause him to examine what kind of person he is, or aspires to be. The question should then be followed by a truthful statement such as, "That's one of the things that I've always respected about you," or, "I've always admired people who aren't afraid to take a chance."

Phrases like these are effective in two ways: they reshape his self-image to include the definition of someone who holds these values, and it prevents his own objection at a later point, as he has already stated that it is important to forgive.

Then broach the subject with Danny when he's in a good mood, excited, or looking forward to something:

"I was speaking with Yitzi and he is just devastated by what he did. He's barely been eating. You should know that he's been in counseling ever since—two days a week for now. He's really ashamed of his behavior towards you and others."

Remember to let Danny know that he can dictate the terms of the conversation and that he can choose the "where" and "when"; or if practical, set up a place and time yourself, whereby Danny would have to proactively cancel in order to avoid going. Perhaps too, have him speak with someone whom he respects who was in a similar situation, and who sought to make peace.

18

Help to Settle a Deadlock in Mediation, Arbitration, or Negotiation

Research in this area reveals some intriguing insights into how to best help others to resolve their differences. Four prevailing laws of human nature are always at work and are responsible for tilting the conflict toward either resolution or escalation.

Law 1: The Law of Scarcity

Would you like a free diamond ring? Or maybe you would prefer an aluminum can? Which do you want *more*, and *why*? Obviously, the ring, as it is perceived as more valuable because of the degree of availability in relation to demand. It is our innate drive to want what is rare, to want what we cannot have, and to appreciate more what we have worked for. So how do you apply the law of scarcity in these types of conflicts?

If you are a mediator, this law is effectively harnessed by reducing the expectations of both sides, and showing each party that their options are limited. Options provide leverage.

And if each side believes that he can get a better deal by going elsewhere or waiting, you will not resolve the dispute. Only when both parties recognize that they will lose more if they delay can you expect cooperation.

Everything in life has deadlines or expiration dates. From coupons to our own existence (we don't live forever), deadlines force action. It is human nature to often procrastinate until conditions become more favorable or until we are in a better mood before we take action. To avoid this emotional hurdle, give a clear-cut deadline and let the person know that the action must be taken *now*, because he won't have a chance to do so later.

This also incorporates another psychological principle: we don't like our freedom to be restricted. By letting him know that he may not get the opportunity to act in the future, he will assign a greater value to the offer, and will move more quickly to preserve it.

Law 2: The Law of Contrast and Comparison

It doesn't matter whether you're dividing up assets or negotiating a contract—everybody wants their fair share.[1]

Is $300 a fair price for a watch? It's hard to say. But if you told me that it was originally on sale for $1,600, I would (perhaps erroneously) assume that $300 is fair. The degree to which we are *satisfied* with what we get depends mostly on the law of contrast and comparison.

1. Seeking a fair resolution is a Torah principle. For example the verse states, "You must do what is fair [*yashar*] and good in the eyes of God" (*Devarim* 6:18). Rashi (ad loc.) comments, "This refers to compromise and going beyond the letter of the law." The Ramban (ad loc.) notes that this verse is a general directive to do what is "good and fair," since it is impossible for the Torah to specify correct behavior in all situations relating to one's neighbors, friends, business, communities and countries.

Q In what situation can you give someone the moon and they would still not be satisfied?

A If there are three moons and the other guy got two of them. "How come he gets two moons? That's not fair!"

If each side feels that he is being taken advantage of, the situation will not be resolved anytime soon. This is true from land deals to union contracts to severance packages. It all comes down to, "What am *I* getting and what will it do for *me*?" versus, "What are *they* getting and what will it do for *them*?"

The *ultimatum game* reveals an interesting insight into human nature.[2] In one such demonstration of the theory,[3] researchers offered random strangers the opportunity to participate in a one-time game. Each person was paired with a random partner, whose identity would not be revealed, and put into separate rooms. Here's how the game worked: each pair was given one hundred dollars, but the twist was that one person (of the pair) was arbitrarily chosen to split the money any way he wanted. However, the receiving partner could then either accept or reject the offer; if the offer was rejected, both would leave empty-handed. In the majority of instances when less than 50 dollars was offered, the person rejected the money and preferred to walk away with nothing rather than feel that he had been taken advantage of. Justice was served.

---

2. The ultimatum game is the brainchild of Israeli game theorist Ariel Rubinstein, who accurately predicted in 1982 that the person asked to decide in such a game would choose to offer the least amount possible.

3. W. Güth, R. Schmittberger, & B. Schwarze, "An Experimental Analysis of Ultimatum Bargaining," *Journal of Economic Behavior and Organization* 3(4) (1982), pp. 367–388.

Seek Compromise

In the absence of an agreement by the parties, arbitration by a *Beis Din* takes the form of compromise or settlement in accordance with Jewish law (*pesharah krovah l'din*).[4] In effect, the Mishnah advises judges to apply *pesharah* (compromise) first, and only turn to *din* (the strict letter of the law) should the parties refuse to cooperate.[5]

We know that envy is an intolerable trait because it is rooted in a lack of trust in God—that somehow someone else got what should have been yours; therein lies the desire to compare.[6] The reality is that we all have the precise measure of what we need for our individual growth and wellbeing. In *Mesilas Yesharim*, we learn that: "Envy, too, is nothing but lack of reason and foolishness, for the one who envies gains nothing for himself and deprives the one he envies of nothing. He only loses thereby, as is indicated in the verse that I mentioned (*Iyov* 5:2), 'Envy kills the fool.'"[7]

The Torah states: "They shall judge the people at all times, and they shall bring every major matter to you, and every minor matter they shall judge, and it will be eased for you, and they shall bear you. If you do this thing—and God shall command

---

4.   *Shulchan Aruch, Choshen Mishpat* 12:2.

5.   *Sanhedrin* 6b.

6.   Acting on one's envy by compelling the owner to sell the item to him, transgresses one of the Ten Commandments, "Do not covet" (*Shemos* 20:13). Cf. *Sefer HaMitzvos, Lo sa'aseh* 265, 266).

7.   Rabbi Moshe Chaim Luzzato, *Mesilas Yesharim*, ch. 11.

you—then you will be able to endure, and this entire people, as well, shall arrive at its destination in peace."[8]

A recent commentary to this verse affirms, "When people are confident that they are ruled justly, they are at peace, free from resentment and frustration, for people can more easily cope with problems and poverty than with the feeling that more powerful or better connected individuals are taking advantage of them. Indeed the blessing of *Shemoneh Esrei* that asks for the restoration of justice includes the related plea, '. . . and remove us from sorrow and groan,' for with justice comes contentment."[9]

Anger is a destructive force, but takes an even worse turn when it boils into our relationships. An enraged ego is envious (it desires what others have) and jealous (it fears that others will take what it has).

Themes of jealousy and envy appear several times in the Biblical narrative. Kayin was jealous of Hevel, Eisav of Yaakov, Rachel of Leah, and the brothers of Yosef.[10] Jealousy also plagued King Shaul's relationship with David. Each of these junctures was a pivotal point in Jewish history. These destructive emotions run deep and pervade many facets of our lives. As our Sages remind us, "Jealousy, lust, and honor remove man from the world,"[11] and, "Envy causes the bones to rot."[12]

---

8. *Shemos* 18:22–23.

9. *The Chumash*, Stone Edition (NY: Artscroll/Mesorah Publications, August 2001), ad loc.

10. The brothers had long-harbored resentment towards Yosef, but their plot to kill him did not begin until their feelings turned to envy for their father's affection.

11. *Pirkei Avos* 4:21.

12. *Mishlei* 14:30, as explained by *Metzudos*.

What we deem as fair is largely irrational; and as unusual as it might seem, we generally are less consumed with what we get as long as we don't feel that we're being taken advantage of—that would be disrespectful.

Similar Means Relatable

The Ramchal writes, " 'Every craftsman hates his fellow.' We are envious of those who are more similar to us. Even though others are wealthier, more powerful, and respected, it is we who become the target of the insecure neighbor because he can more easily identify with us. He has no quarrel with those out of the league of his imagination."[13]

Law 3: The Law of Reciprocity

Have you ever been in a situation where someone does something for you, and you feel uncomfortable unless you can pay him back in some way? We know we don't *have* to, but we often feel uneasy until we can reciprocate—we are reluctant to feel dependant on another person. As we mentioned in the beginning of the book, we need to achieve a sense of independence in order to have self-respect.

Any side that *gives in* to the other creates a sense of dependency in the other side. A concession that one side makes pulls the other—unconsciously—closer to the middle. If both sides are unwilling to compromise, it means that the psychological

---

13. *Bereishis Rabbah* 19:4, as quoted in Rabbi Moshe Chaim Luzzato. *Mesilas Yesharim*, ch. 11.

law of reciprocity is not engaged, and cooperation from either side is unlikely.

Law 4: The Law of Rational Response

If someone is emotionally charged, particularly with anger, there is little hope of reaching a concession or compromise.

Careful attention should be paid to ensure that there is no added animosity from either side. Shouting, slanderous statements, and gestures of animosity will cause greater hostility as well as a host of Torah prohibitions. When hostility is reduced, there is a greater chance that a satisfactory agreement will be reached.

Get Smart

If you remove the people and the personalities from the equation and look only at the facts, you eliminate the majority of obstacles. It is for this reason that it is advisable to meet with each party separately, at least initially, to best gauge where you are and what needs to be done in order to effectively approach the situation.

Real-Life Scenarios

While there are a multitude of variables in each and every scenario, we'll take a case of where you are mediating the severance package between Chaim and his employers.

You need to make each party aware of the other's options. For instance, the company should know that Chaim has legal resources—if, of course, this is true. At the same time, Chaim needs to know that the company will shortly be laying off more people, and that if this case is not resolved now, it will get lost in a sea of others. By emphasizing that no one benefits by delay, you greatly enhance the chance of resolution.

Furthermore, if each party comes in with no room to negotiate, each will be seen as unyielding, and the law of reciprocity will never be engaged. Therefore, give each side wiggle room in order to make concessions and build positive momentum. Chaim should be told to come in with a reasonable demand, but with the awareness that he will have to make some concessions. This engages the law of contrast/comparison as well as the law of reciprocity. And during the negotiations, he should be respectful to all and encouraged not to become emotionally entangled. To be clear, being passionate about one's cause is well and good, but once it spills over into hostility, you have begun to harm the process.

Whether you are mediating a workplace conflict or a family dispute, the goal of course, should not only be to resolve the conflict, but to help foster a cordial and more productive relationship between the parties.

19

Bring People Closer Together, Who Have Either Grown Apart or Who Just Don't Get Along

The Zohar (Parshas Emor) explains that the children of Aharon were selected for the priesthood because Aharon was a person who was known for bringing peace between husbands and wives and between neighbors and friends. If Aharon saw two people quarreling he would wait, and then go privately to each of them, and tell him how the other is hurting and in great pain over the fallout. Then, when the two people saw each other again, they would have warm feelings and reconcile.

It doesn't much matter if any one person is at fault, because the one who is responsible clearly doesn't see it this way. We can assume there was a difference of opinion over who did what to whom and who is to blame for what. Or it may be just a general lack of respect for one another, manifesting itself in conversations filled with sarcastic remarks and an underlying air of hostility, competition, or jealousy.

Your overall objective is to give information about each party to the other—information that will change how each

person sees the other and consequently how each person inter-
acts with and treats the other.

Phase 1: Reestablish Respect

Let each person know that the other one really respects the way
he does a particular thing, or how the other admires something
that he stands for or supports. In almost every situation, the
reason one person treats the other with a lack of respect is simply
that he doesn't feel that he gets respect from the other person.
You will find almost every single time that each person—who
now feels respected by the other—begins to express greater
tolerance and even kindness for the other.

Phase 2: Demonstrate Consequences

Let each one know that while the other didn't say anything to
you outright, you know that each cares a great deal about what
the other thinks of him, and he might want to lighten up a bit.
Suggest too, that each one give the other some nice words of
encouragement, as you know that these words will go a long
way and make the other feel good.

Phase 3: Humanize

Because anonymity lessens inhibitions, human beings are
capable of inflicting the most pain—whether emotional
or physical—when our identities are hidden. As part of an
experiment, behavioral psychologist Phillip Zimbardo dressed
New York University women all in white coats and hoods. They
were asked to give "electric shocks" to an individual. (Of course

the shocks weren't real, but the participants believed that they were.) The masked women pressed the shock button twice as long as did another group of women who were not masked and wearing clearly visible name tags.[1]

Further research demonstrates that when we cannot see the person, either by being able to identify the person physically or relate to him emotionally, our ability to feel empathy is compromised. For this reason the psychological trauma for a pilot who drops a bomb on a city will often be less than for a ground soldier who has had to shoot a man at point-blank range.

It's good to let the other know things—as long as it doesn't violate one's trust and confidence in the other. When we learn that someone had a tragedy when young, or is suffering from an illness, we can't help but be more compassionate.[2]

In most cases one of the people is really causing most of the friction, so you would want to focus your efforts on him.

---

1. P. G. Zimbardo, "The Human Choice: Individuation, Reason, and Order Versus Deindividuation, Impulse, and Chaos," In W. J. Arnold and D. Levine (Eds.), 1969 *Nebraska Symposium on Motivation*. University of Nebraska Press (1970), pp. 237–307.

2. To avoid speaking *lashon hara* (derogatory speech) about the person's problem, one should first gain permission to reveal such information. If this is not possible, then the following conditions have to be met for it to be classified as constructive speech (*Chafetz Chaim, Hilchos Lashon Hara* 10:2, quoted in *Journey to Virtue* 21:2–4):

1. The information is true and was witnessed by you.
2. You gave constructive criticism to the subject before revealing it to others.
3. You must not exaggerate the wrongdoing.
4. Your intention must be purely and entirely beneficial.
5. It is impossible to achieve the same benefit by other means.
6. You are certain that revealing the information will not lead to the subject being damaged further.

Us Against Them

Numerous studies conclude that division among people dissolves when there is an opposing outside threat. Civil war, intersocietal conflicts, and internal unrest often cease when a common outside enemy comes onto the scene. Conversely, individuals more often will turn their attention and hostility to one another when no outside forces are present. The fastest way to instill cooperation between two people is to (a) create an external focus and/or (b) simply set your group against another group in some form of healthy competition.

Real-Life Scenarios

A school principal has two teachers who don't get along well. He's not sure what caused the problem, and he doesn't believe he'd get a straight answer if he asked. He simply wants to get them to become friendlier and work together better. (Teacher 1 is the cause of most of the friction.)

Principal to Teacher 1

Principal: "I've got to tell you, I know that you and Teacher 2 don't always see eye-to-eye on things, but I think some of the remarks you made really upset her."

Teacher 1: "Really? I didn't say anything that rude. Maybe she's just sensitive."

Principal: "I know, but I happen to know that she has a great deal of respect for you, and the comments sting a bit when they come from someone she really just wants to impress."

Teacher 1: "Oh, okay. I never realized."

Principal: "I know. So any words of encouragement are going to mean an awful lot to her. Besides, she's been through a lot with her son, who's been in and out of the hospital for the past few years."

Principal to Teacher 2

Principal: "You know, I was speaking with Teacher 1 about the upcoming parent conference and she suggested that I ask you for your thoughts."

[He solicits her insight and then adds] "I know that you and Teacher 1 have had your moments, but she thinks you're an excellent teacher."

The Rift: When They Drifted Apart Over Something Minor or Now Irrelevant

In these situations the catalyst is gone. Either what caused the rift was something minor that was blown out of proportion or what once was an issue is no longer relevant. What's left are just hurt feelings.

Phase 1: Reestablish Good Feelings

Ideally, you want to reestablish the relationship in the thoughts of each person, meaning that you bring each one back into the other person's life—first in their mind. Since some time has passed, the relationship may not be taking center stage in their lives. And if they are not thinking about each other, they don't feel as if they are missing anything. Using one or more of the following routes will help to get the mental ball rolling.

- To each person, tell a humorous or touching story about the two of them, from the "good old days."

- Let each person know that the other was asking or always asks how the other is doing and is concerned when things are not going well.
- Reestablish mutual respect by letting each one know that the other speaks well of him and often praises his actions, lifestyle, choices, and so on.

Phase 2: Try for a Fast Solution

Now you gauge the situation to see if you can end this fast. To one of the people, say the following:

> "Jon is very sorry for what happened and regrets that the two of you are not speaking. I know that if you made the first move and called, he would be eager to hear from you. After so much time, he feels so bad and can't bring himself to call."

Next, if he agrees, then skip to Phase 7 and continue from there. If he does not, then go to the other person with the same technique. If the other person agrees, then continue to Phase 7. If neither one agrees, then read on.

Phase 3: One More Try

Before you abandon this option, if neither will commit to calling, see how either feels about writing a letter or having you call with a message from him. Anything that begins to build momentum is positive and productive. If you still have no success at this point, continue with Phase 4.

Phase 4: The Crowbar

You want to see if either person is simply putting up a strong front. This technique will help you to decide whether the person is or isn't really interested in reestablishing the relationship—as well as to decide which one will be likely to yield first.

Tell the person that she has to agree to doing what you ask, but only if you can achieve some highly difficult and amazing task. For instance, you would ask her to think of a number from one to one hundred and if you can guess what it is then she will agree to hearing you out and/or agreeing to make peace. She will probably agree, because she believes that there is little chance that you can guess right. If she does not agree to these terms, then it is likely that she is adamant about her stance. In doing this you accomplish several things—most notably being able to determine who is going to be the one who will need a harder sell and who is more likely to consider mending fences. If both readily agree, then you know you've got an easier job.

The objective here is not in being right, although if you are that's great. Rather, it's in her agreeing to take the chance. Again, if at this point she absolutely refuses, then you know what you're up against. But if she does agree, then you've managed to adjust her belief system slightly—and this is all you need. You take her from a 'no' to a 'maybe.'

Now she will have to alter her belief system to allow the possibility—though remote—for a reunion to happen. In order to reduce dissonance, she unconsciously adjusts her thinking and will now become more open. Only someone who in the back of her mind is willing to make peace would take part in this test. So some part of her, to some degree, is willing to make peace. Now you know that you're not faced with an impossible task.

Phase 5: Gathering Ammunition and Icebreakers

Now you know that you're dealing with willing participants, so you need to gather firepower that you can use. If the two people keep saying why they are mad and why they hate the other and that they want nothing to do with the other, then their thoughts are locked into a stubborn rut. To change this, ask a series of questions that move them into the frame of making peace. Ask questions such as:

- "What would you have done differently?"
- "Do you regret how things have turned out?"
- "If you could erase that day, would you?"
- "What did you enjoy from the relationship?"
- "Do you remember any of the good times?"

What these questions do is give you ammunition for two objectives. One, is when you go to each person and say that the other said, "He wishes he could erase that day," or "He regrets how things have turned out," you have room to create a resolution.

The other is when you go to the next stage of planning the outcome, you want to be sure that each person is armed with something to say to break the ice. Ask each person, "What would you have to hear from the other to begin to talk again?" The answers to these questions give you such icebreakers such as, "I'm sorry how things unfolded," or "I never should have provoked you."

This gives you the opportunity to see where the answer to this question blends in with the answers to each of the above questions. "I shouldn't have said what I did," can be easily translated into an apology if one is listening for it.

Phase 6: What Will It Take?

Now that they are in the right mental mode, ask, "What would you have to hear from the other person to begin to talk again?" Or, "What would he have to do to begin to make things right?" Then, whatever it is, see if the other person is willing to agree to his request. You just may be surprised at what one asks, and what one is willing to do.

If you get a reasonable response from one or both, then proceed to the next phase. Note: It's important to emphasize to each person that the other is excited and thankful to be able to put this behind him. Knowing that the other person is eager to reconcile helps both people focus on the relationship and not on the conflict.

Phase 7: Plan the Outcome

When you get them to agree to talk, make sure you plan it out. You take care of all the details. Don't say, "Just meet somewhere and talk it out." You arrange everything and, most important, confer with each person about what he will say to the other when they first meet. Ideally, each person should be readied with the following:

A. Whether it's an apology of some sort or the expression of a willingness to listen or an expression of regret, you need to have the icebreakers ready to go or you risk an uncomfortable conversation marred with standoffish behavior. Take the answers you get from Phase 5 to prepare each person with something positive to say.

and/or

B. If you can't think of icebreakers that you like or can use, remember that your overall objective is to get each person to see the situation from the other's point of view. Therefore, let each person know why the other did what he did and have that person reiterate it when they meet. For instance, "I know that you got so upset with me because you had my best interest at heart." This validates each person's actions.

These two ideas are gentle ways of saying and showing that each person is interested in reestablishing the relationship.

Phase 8: Wrap Up After the Fact

Once there is a reconciliation, sometimes buyer's remorse sets in. This is a term used in sales when the buyer has second thoughts about his purchase. The same thing could easily happen here, where one person thinks, "Did I make a fool of myself?" or "Did he take me seriously?" etc. Therefore, it is up to you to seal the process by letting each person know—individually, of course—that the other person feels great about what has taken place and how the renewed friendship and/or relationship has made him happy.

Real-Life Scenarios

Two mothers-in-law got into an argument over the wedding of their children and have not spoken for three years. The children—son and daughter—want them to reconcile.

Child To Each Mother

"I was speaking to my mother-in-law and she reminded me of the story of when you two went shopping for the wedding dress and got locked in the dressing room. You know, whenever I speak to her, she's always asking about you. And when you were sick that time, she must have called a half-dozen times to check on how you were."

[Quick settle] "She feels just awful that the two of you are not speaking, and for what happened. I know that if you called, she would love to hear from you. After so much time, she feels so bad and is too embarrassed to call."

[Second try] "If you'll let me, I'll call her and set it up. Why don't we all go to lunch, and put this nonsense behind us? I know she'd like that."

The children proceed to Phase 4 to gather icebreakers for when the mothers meet. They ask questions such as, "Let me ask you this: Do you have any regrets how things turned out?" Or, "What would you have done differently?"

The children arrange for everyone to meet, arming each person with something to say. For instance, Mother 1 would be asked to say that she missed the relationship, and Mother 2 would be told that it would be good for her to say that she is sorry for how things got out of hand.

Then the children secure the reunion afterward by letting each mother know that the other really enjoys being on good terms again and is grateful for the reunion.

21

When Nothing Seems to Work: Six Tactics for Dealing With the Most Challenging of People and Situations

A ny one, or more, of the following six tactics can be used in intractable situations, and implemented by an impartial third party.[1] Once you have made the most of one or more of these techniques, employ the strategies outlined in the appropriate chapter.

Emergency Tactic 1: A Dose of Reality

Have you ever driven by a bad traffic accident and noticed that the passengers in your car suddenly become *nicer* to one another? There's a sort of quiet kindness that permeates.

---

1. The following is quoted from Aryeh Kaplan, *The Handbook of Jewish Thought*, vol. 2 (Brooklyn, NY: Moznaim Publishing Corp., 1979), 17:46: "It is preferable to seek forgiveness by oneself rather than through an intermediary (*Machatzis HaShekel* to Siman 606). However, if it is difficult to do so alone, or if there is more likelihood in gaining forgiveness, one may request the assistance of an intermediary (*Mishnah Berurah* 606:2; *Kitzur Shulchan Aruch* 131:4)."

Have you ever been to visit a friend at the hospital, and the second you walk out the lobby doors you look around and see the world just a little bit differently? You feel a mixture of relief, sadness, and optimism. In essence, the experience produces a *shift in perspective*. You feel happy to be alive and grateful for what you have.

For one or both parties to experience this emotional shift, take each one, always separately, to the hospital, a funeral home, or similar setting in order to jolt them back into reality.

Studies confirm that people are more charitable and forgiving after they have spent some time contemplating their own mortality.[2] You want them to recognize what is really important, but unfortunately, the effect of such exposure wears off very quickly. So strike while the iron is hot; have each side commit then and there to arranging a set date to meet.

Emergency Tactic 2: Your Swan Song

If you reveal to each side some sort of recent tragedy or hardship—for example, your goldfish died, your house burned down, you were diagnosed with an illness—then someone who does not want to add to your distress will most likely acquiesce to your request. Furthermore, he will realize that if you are choosing to get involved, despite everything that has happened to you, the issue must be important to you, and he will not wish to disappoint you further.

Emphasize that he is not doing it for the other person, or even for himself, *but for you*. Even if you don't think that you

---

2.   E. Jonas, J. Schimel, J. Greenberg, and T. Pyszczynski, "The Scrooge Effect: Evidence that Mortality Salience Increases Prosocial Attitudes and Behavior," *Personality and Social Psychology Bulletin* 28:10 (2002), pp. 1342–1353.

hold enough sway, the approach can still be effective because you're shifting his motivation.

Let's say that you're an unemployed person who plans to attend a job fair. You might feel a little self-conscious. But now let's imagine a different scenario. You are conducting research on the crisis in the job market, and you are attending the event for the purpose of research. In this context, your self-consciousness evaporates, because *it's not about you*, it's about your assignment. Your ego isn't on the line. In much the same way, making peace between two people sometimes involves *removing them* from the equation and directing their focus to someone or something else.

Emergency Tactic 3: God is Sending Me a Message

When someone refuses to listen to you or others, there is one source or entity that he will listen to: God. If he feels that the Creator of the *universe* is trying to tell him something, he may be more receptive. He won't listen to you or anyone else, but God—that is a different story.

Ask him to be on the lookout for signs that God wants him to reconcile, apologize, or listen. If he subconsciously wants to make peace, this will give him the emotional permission that he needs, and he will begin to see signs.

As we learned, what we choose to focus on determines what we see. To illustrate how this phenomenon works, let's look at an example from one's day-to-day life. Did you ever purchase a new car only to find afterwards that many others were driving the same car as you? Or were you ever thinking about an old friend, and then kept running into people that looked like him?

The idea presented above coincides with the laws of

attraction, whereby our thoughts help to manifest the reality that unfolds. So not only will this person be more receptive to making peace, but he will help to foster the optimum conditions that will help make this possible.

Emergency Tactic 4: It's Too Late for Me, but Not for You

There is no shortage of people who would give their life savings to have a five-minute conversation with someone who has passed on.

Ask one of these people who never had the chance to reconcile with someone in his life to speak to one or both of those involved in the conflict. The suffering caused by not being able to make things right can be enormous. Therefore, you will be doing all the people involved a great favor. Even for the person who has lost his chance, explaining and conveying to someone else the importance of forgiveness will often help alleviate some of his own guilt (and possibly complete his *teshuvah*).[3] This is a useful method in getting one person to at least hear the other out.

Emergency Tactic 5: Reshuffling the Deck

Use any significant event in either of the sides' lives as a launching pad for peace. Positive or negative, whether a *bris*, special

---

3.   If the person against whom one has transgressed has died, he should bring ten people to the person's grave and declare, "I have sinned against God and against this person whom I have wronged." The people assembled then answer three times, "You are forgiven." (See *Shulchan Aruch, Orach Chaim* 606:2, and *Mishnah Berurah*, ad loc. for more details.) If he cannot go himself to the person's grave, then he may have an agent gather ten people at the gravesite and make the declaration on his behalf. (Cf. *Mishnah Berurah* 606:14).

kiddush or wedding, or a funeral or *yahrtzeit,* events such as these cause the emotional deck to be reshuffled. You will have a better chance at drawing a new hand. During these critical life-cycle moments, our values and priorities become realigned. This provides the perfect opportunity to open up the gateways of communication.

Any action—a phone call, card, or gift—that acknowledges a crisis or a cause for celebration is one of the simplest yet most effective methods to reestablish contact.

Emergency Tactic 6: Let's Go

When you have leverage but you are out of options, consider taking the person with you without discussing or informing beforehand. As long as you don't feel that the meeting will become explosive, a face-to-face encounter may perhaps stir strong postive feelings and prompt an end to the conflict. As well, providing one party with the opportunity to make his case as to why the other is wrong may serve as a tempting incentive for a get-together. Even though the meeting is bound to be tumultuous, which is far from ideal, at least you've got them in the same room.

PART **5**

Harmony at Home

The Key to
Shalom Bayis (Family Harmony)

A s life becomes increasingly more comfortable and conve-
nient, we fall out of the habit of exerting ourselves; and
the idea of investing effort into a relationship—even if it is with
someone we care for—is becoming increasingly foreign. As a
result we have become accustomed to the notion that comfort
is the path to happiness. (Or perhaps more damaging is the
notion that comfort *is* happiness.)

As we look at this issue through the lens of Torah, it is obvious that we're becoming a generation of takers instead of givers.
Therefore, if you are accustomed to being in a taking mode,
it will prove to be very difficult to make concessions in your
marriage.

Parenthetically, when it comes to our young children, we
demonstrate a far greater capacity to give. It is often easier to
give unconditional love to your child than to your spouse. The
reason is tied in to our beliefs. We *expect* our spouse to give,
whereas children are supposed to take.

If we are filled with resentment as a result of our sense of
entitlement, we will inevitably feel miserable and take our

spouse right along with us. Rabbi E. Dessler highlights this point when he writes, "When demands begin, love departs."[1]

Sometimes, it can be very difficult for us to give in, because it seems like we have to relinquish a part of ourselves, rendering us vulnerable. But the truth is that by conceding, ultimately you win. "Giving in" is not about being selfless, but about being *sensible*. Not only have you done something tremendous for your *shalom bayis* and for your character, but your action will produce a consequence that will result in *your* maximum benefit.

It does not matter whether you lease or buy a car, what the kids have for supper, or who sits where for Shabbos. If you think that you can be truly happy when your spouse is miserable, you have made a mistake.[2]

When I ask couples to consider this point, one person, usually the man, will customarily say, "But I'm right! In this case, I happen to be right. I looked at the facts, I looked at the numbers, it all makes sense." And with as much compassion as I can muster, with as much sympathy as I can express, my response is, "What does it matter?" You can be right or you can be happy. You can't always be both.

Our happiness is not contingent upon things we get, or even on our experiences. Rather, only the quality of our choices determines our satisfaction with life, and for that matter, the entirety of our relationships and wellbeing.

---

1. "I always say to a couple at their wedding: 'Make sure, my dear ones, that you always desire to give happiness and pleasure to one another, as you feel at this time. And know, that the moment that you start making demands from each other—behold, your happiness has already left you.' " (Rabbi Eliyahu Dessler, "On the Love between a Man and Wife," *Kuntres HaChessed*, p. 39).

2. There are times, however, when giving in is inappropriate. Your spouse may not be seeing reality clearly, or may have a weakness on a certain issue, as we all do in many areas of life at some point or another. In such a situation, sit down and talk it out, using the strategy in the following chapter.

Shalom—peace—is the only vehicle through which blessing comes down to earth from Heaven.[3] By making peace the
priority, whenever you find yourselves heading for a disagreement or conflict, the decision about the correct way to proceed
is made easier for you: intrinsically, whatever brings peace into
the home is what will make us happy.[4]

Furthermore, Rabban Shimon ben Gamliel says that a person
who brings peace into his house is considered by God as if he
brought peace to the entire Jewish people.[5]

Don't Some Things Matter?

What the children eat will affect their health; the car
that we buy may not be as safe as another model; and
who we invite over for Shabbos will affect our enjoy-
ment. We could go on and on, but the bottom line is
that as long as the circumstance does not require an
open miracle, trust that God will make it work out for
the best—whether or not it is readily observable—
because God Himself tells us that He wants peace. So
much so that the Torah permits the holy Name of God

---

3.   Rabbi Shimon ben Chalafta said, "*The only vessel that God could find to contain
the blessings of Israel was shalom* (peace), as it is written: 'God will give strength
to His people; God will bless His nation with peace' (*Tehillim* 29:11)" (*Mishnah
Uktzin* 3:12).

4.   There is a difference of opinion about the proper way to affix the Mezuzah.
Rashi (*Menachos* 33b) rules that it should be set horizontally, while Rabbeinu Tam
(*ibid.*) rules that it should be set vertically. Diagonal is acceptable according to
both, and this is the accepted custom in many communities (*Rema, Yoreh De'ah*
389:6). The *mezuzah* thus serves as a reminder that *shalom bayis* trumps who is
right and who is wrong. The Gemara also teaches that even when you feel that
you are entirely in the right, it is better to seek to compromise (*Bava Metzia* 88a).

5.   *Avos d'Rebbi Nosson* 28:3.

to be erased in water (in the course of the *Sotah* ritual) in order to restore peace to the relationship between husband and wife (*Chullin* 141a; *Nedarim* 66b). Even a public vow that cannot normally be annulled, can be annulled in order to maintain peace between spouses (Rema, *Yoreh De'ah* 228:21).

Masters of Our Destiny

It's all too easy to observe other people's relationships and presume that they have the ideal marriage and partnership. In reality, though, every couple faces challenges.

Each marriage has its own set of unique circumstances, but every married couple has one basic choice when it comes to responding to their challenges. The all-too common response is to get frustrated and disappointed when painful challenges appear. Then we begin to identify the other as the source of our own unhappiness and begin to try to change *them*; and if we are unsuccessful, as we are likely to be, our feelings for our spouse begin to wane.

Harboring such feelings towards your spouse can manifest itself in the realm of action, with complaints, criticism, and even acts of revenge. If this process continues far enough, the negative feelings within the marriage (resentment and contempt) can destroy the relationship—leading either to divorce or estrangement.

Couples who are aware that the answer to most of their marital challenges lies within themselves, are able to make the better choice when faced with these difficulties.

There is almost always, in every marriage, a situation where at least one side has a significant character flaw and might not be living up to his or her marital responsibilities. As a result, it is common to hear the other side protest, "He is not fulfilling his responsibility so I will not fulfill mine." According to the Torah, however, just because your spouse is neglecting his or her role doesn't mean that you are absolved of your obligations.[6]

We are in this world in order to grow. The challenges that accompany married life should therefore be seen as opportunities for growth. To ignore these opportunities, or to take the seemingly easy way out, is not only foolish and irresponsible, but is ultimately detrimental to our emotional and spiritual well-being.

From a Position of Strength

If we concede out of fear or guilt, this does nothing to enhance self-esteem; it only diminishes it. It is not really us giving; it is the other person taking. We are being taken advantage of with our consent. We know that in our own lives, when someone tries to guilt us into doing something and we stand up for ourselves and say "No," we feel better about ourselves. This is the same type of empowerment felt when we say "Yes" to a request that we should be accommodating, but are not in the mood to do so. Whatever our response, as long as it is from a position of strength—meaning we choose our course of action—we are victorious.

---

6. In cases where abuse is involved, a person has the obligation to protect their own physical and emotional wellbeing. Your marital responsibilities don't include being a victim. See page 66, note 8, for more on abusive relationships.

23

Five Foundations of a Successful Marriage

Beyond a change in outlook, there are practical, specific steps that can be taken to improve your marriage. Following are five rules which are utilized by successful, happy, and fulfilled couples.

Choosing a Candle

If a person cannot afford to buy both a candle for Shabbos and wine for *Kiddush*, a Shabbos candle takes precedence. Similarly, if a person cannot afford to buy a candle for Shabbos and a candle for Chanukah, a Shabbos candle takes precedence; because of peace in the house, for there is no peace without light (which the Shabbos or Yom tov candle provides.) (*Shulchan Aruch, Orach Chaim* 263:3).

Foundation 1: How to Communicate With Your Spouse

Although disagreements are natural in a marriage, when there is a breakdown in communication, unresolved friction creates ill will, and the marriage begins to disintegrate.

The single biggest marriage killer is resentment. Resentment is frozen anger from the past that continues to rear its head today. If something is persistently distressing you, you have to tell your spouse.[1] Your spouse is not a mind-reader. Often, people expect their spouses to know what to do, without having to be told, but it is this type of flawed thinking that leads us down a tumultuous path.

It is important to realize that we do not enter marriage with a deep awareness of what it is that our partner needs. Many issues and particular areas of sensitivity are learned along the way. It is for this reason that openness is crucial. That being said, we need to be careful in how we convey our feelings to our spouse. The following four rules should be followed when we communicate with our spouse.

Before giving criticism of any sort, though, we should be certain that we are not projecting our own faults unto our spouse. Because our spouse serves as our spiritual mirror and messenger, once we have corrected the flaw within ourselves or acknowledge the lesson to be learned, we will find that our spouse adjusts him or herself accordingly, and automatically. Those

---

1. If we do not speak up when necessary, we may act out where inappropriate. Pent-up anger turns into contempt if not properly vented. "He who conceals his hatred has lying lips" (*Mishlei* 10:18). Nonetheless, please see Chapter 6 for additional insights and strategies, and remember that direct criticism between husband and wife should be a last resort.

who seek to educate, improve, and refine their spouse through criticism, labor under a false and destructive impression.[2]

I. Wait 24 Hours. "Do not rush to begin a quarrel."[3] If something continues to trouble you, it is advised to communicate your feelings—but let a little time pass first; as we stated before, time gives us greater clarity because our ego is less engaged and we are able to view the situation with greater objectivity.[4] This is why you are more likely to become irritated in the heat of an argument. After a few moments, your anger will generally begin to subside. Then, a few hours later, you are even less angry, and after a few days, you may find yourself wondering why you were even upset in the first place.

II. Pick Your Time. According to research, people who are in a good mood are more likely to purchase a lottery ticket.[5] When we are joyful, we tend to be more optimistic and are open to possibilities.[6] Try not to allow your desire to speak your

---

2. The unique emotional and spiritual roles of husbands and wives are quite different, and beyond the scope of this work.

3. *Mishlei* 25:8

4. "He spoke to Korach and to his entire assembly, saying 'In the morning Hashem will make known the one who is His own . . .' " (*Bamidbar* 16:5). Rashi comments that by telling Korach and his followers that God would respond in the morning, Moshe sought to give them time to reconsider their thinking.

5. H. R. Arkes, L.T. Herren, and A. M. Isen, "The Role of Potential Loss in the Influence of Affect on Risk-Taking Behavior," *Organizational Behavior and Human Decision Processes* 41 (1988), pp. 181–193.

6. While numerous studies confirm that forgiveness reduces anxiety and depression, and increases self-esteem, research also shows that people in a good mood tend to be more forgiving. In one experiment, participants in positive moods reported more forgiveness than participants in negative moods. (See Alyssa Nguyen, M.A., *Forgiveness: what's mood got to do with it?* Thesis in Psychology, Humboldt State University, 2008.)

Not all negative states create an inhospitable environment for peace. Let us clarify the difference between two emotional states: *mad* and *sad*. The former is a manifestation of the ego, while the latter is an expression of our soul. Someone

mind derail your ability to successfully plan your approach.

Wait until you're both in a positive mood, so you both have the capacity to *give*. When we're in a bad mood or constricted state, we are only capable of taking, making it impossible to see the situation from the other person's perspective. When either one or both of you are hungry, tired, or plainly angry, do not expect that you will have a productive conversation. It's not going to happen too often, if ever.

III. Soften the Start-up. Do not be confrontational when bringing up the problem. Just because the topic is serious doesn't mean that you have to take a dour tone. When we are upset by a situation, it is easy to blame the other person for our feelings, and then project that attitude in the way we communicate. Some people seem to scream what they want and expect to be heard. The volume of our voice does not have to be commensurate with the anger that we feel. On the contrary, when we shout our point, the message is lost. In order for your spouse to be more receptive, your tone of voice should be soft and kind.[7]

IV. Appreciation and Gratitude First. Begin by letting your spouse know that you appreciate all that he or she does for you. Be specific, and sincere in acknowledging how grateful you are

---

feeling sad can be more easily moved to make peace, despite the negativity, because it is not ego-based.

7.   Renowned psychologist and relationship expert, Dr. John Gottman reports, "96 percent of the time you can predict the outcome of a conversation based on the first three minutes of the fifteen-minute interaction. A harsh startup dooms you to failure. The rule is, 'If it starts negative, it stays negative.' " (S. Carrere & J. M. Gottman, "Predicting divorce among newlyweds from the first three minutes of a marital conflict discussion," *Family Process* 38:3 (1999), pp. 293–301).

for all of his or her efforts and hard work. Only in this context, should you then communicate the issue at hand.[8]

Torah Counsel for Husbands

"Be careful to honor your wife, for blessing enters the house only because of the wife" (*Bava Metzia* 59a).

"A man should always take care not to distress his wife, for women's tears are close to the heart of God" (*Bava Metzia* 59a).

"A husband is instructed to honor his wife even more than he honors himself" (*Yevamos* 62b).

Foundation 2: Establish in Advance How to Handle Disagreements

Happy couples know how to gracefully exit a disagreement before it degenerates into a spiteful, vengeful, name-calling discourse. Whatever mechanism you have in place, decide on it ahead of time. Whether it's agreeing to wait a few hours (though a day or two is better), taking a walk, paying your spouse a compliment, changing the topic, or taking some alone time, something must be done to prevent the conversation from devolving into an argument.[9] If you find you are

---

8. If the behavior does not correct itself, your spouse may be thinking, "What's the big deal?!" Accordingly, he or she doesn't take your words seriously. In order for your spouse to validate your feelings, which is ultimately what you are seeking, you may need to gently communicate the *degree* to which you are affected by what is going on.

9. Dr. John Gottman's research shows that an escalation of emotion, which he calls "Diffuse Physiological Arousal (DPA)" creates a physiological change, and we can't think as clearly as we normally do. One of his experiments involved

getting nowhere, stop, or it will cause a needless escalation of unproductive feelings.[10]

Foundation 3: Charity Begins at Home

Gratitude lies at the heart of every relationship: with *ourselves*, God, and fundamentally, with our spouse. A marriage will fall apart quickly if we do not show our loved one adequate appreciation and respect. Absurdly, sometimes we deliver kindness and appreciation to a stranger but disregard the needs of our own spouse, the person who relies on us the most for emotional support.[11]

---

observing couples arguing. When the intensity pushed one of them into a heightened state, Gottman walked into the room and told the couple that his equipment had broken; and asked them to put their discussion on hold for a few minutes until the equipment was repaired. (Nothing was really wrong with the equipment—as researchers they wanted to see what would happen if the couple was given a chance to calm down). As soon as their heart rates dropped closer to normal, Gottman walked back into the room, told them the equipment was fixed, and asked them to pick up their discussion where they left off. The result? "It was as if the couple had a brain transplant," he said, "the tone of the conversation was different. They were more authentic and less guarded—no longer making it personal or taking it so personally. They were more open, and as a result became rational and level-headed." (J. M. Gottman, "Rebound from Marital Conflict and Divorce Prediction," *Family Process* 38 (1999), pp. 287–292).

10.   Researchers at the University of Utah found that couples who have been taught fair-fighting skills have smaller increases in blood pressure when they argue. The lead author Timothy W. Smith, writes, "They learn not to demean or belittle the other person's opinions and not to attack their character. They also learn not to attribute malicious intent to their opponent. They are taught to clearly and effectively express their own feelings about something and to make sure to express an understanding of the other person's point of view before moving on to explaining their own." (T. W. Smith, P. C. Brown, "Cynical Hostility, Attempts to Exert Social Control and Cardiovascular Reactivity in Married Couples," *Journal of Behavioral Medicine* 14 (1991), pp. 581–592

11.   There are principles of precedence that determine to whom one should give one's *tzedakah* money first. These principles apply also to doing acts of loving kindness (Cf. *Ahavas Chessed* 1:6:14). If you perform an act of kindness at the

Does your spouse *have* to cook you dinner? Does your spouse *have* to earn a living? Does your spouse *have* to put the children to bed? Maybe yes, maybe no, the argument is academic. We should not take for granted anything our spouse does for us.

Foundation 4: Stop Bringing Up the Past

"When arguing, focus on the issue at hand."[12] Couples who inject the past into present conversations are not going to move forward in a healthy and constructive fashion. Resolve what can be resolved, and then move on.

Even if you are still bothered by something that your spouse has done in the past, bringing it up only keeps it alive. You have to make a decision to let go of the issue, and once you have made this resolution, you will find that your spouse's past behavior will trouble you less. When you let go of it, it will let go of you. In particular, research shows that forgiveness actually restores positive thoughts, feelings and behaviors toward the offending party. [13]

Foundation 5: Edit Yourself

As insightful and aware as we are, we need not comment on everything that our spouse does that fails to meet with our exacting standards. Could your spouse have done something

---

expense of your marriage, or because you're lacking validation at home, then it is not truly an act of *chessed*. Instead of being a selfless act, it becomes a selfish one.

12. *Mishlei* 25:9.

13. K. A. Lawler, J. W. Younger, R. L. Piferi, R. L. Jobe, K. A. Edmondson, and W. H. Jones, "The Unique Effects of Forgiveness on Health: An Exploration of Pathways," *Journal of Behavioral Medicine* (April 2005).

a little better, smarter, less expensive, easier, faster? Sure, but leave it alone.

You willl notice a different atmosphere when you no longer critique the daily activities of your spouse. Mainly, your spouse may also begin to censor him or herself. Most people are not aware of how often they criticize their spouse, or anyone else in their lives, for that matter.

Have you ever noticed how nice it is to be around someone who is complimentary and sincerely kind and warm? In contrast, have you ever thought about how trying it is to spend five minutes with the person who's always finding fault with everything and everyone? These people seem to drain the life right out of you. Being the person who makes your spouse feel good, will go a long way towards fostering a positive relationship.

Torah Counsel for Wives

"A good wife is a crown to her husband, but one who acts shamefully is like rot in his bones" (Mishlei 12:4).
"It is better to live in a corner of the roof than share a large house with a quarrelsome wife" (Mishlei 21:9).
"A bad wife is like a dreary, rainy day" (Yevamos 63b).

24

Raising Happy, Healthy, and Emotionally Resilient Children

This chapter follows the preceding one because without peace in the home, one cannot hope to raise well-adjusted children.[1] Marital disharmony sets off a chain reaction resulting in generations and generations of children who will (statistically speaking),[2] in their adult lives, unconsciously seek to perpetuate the misery they experienced in their childhood.[3]

The focus of building a productive and loving relationship with one's child centers on building the child's self-esteem. A

---

1. This chapter does not deal with parenting techniques *per se*, but rather focuses primarily on the relationship between the child and parent. Of course, the two issues are not mutually exclusive, but an in-depth examination of parenting—dealing with discipline, behavioral and learning issues, tantrums, and the like—is beyond the scope of this book. The themes presented here deal with self-esteem and independence.

2. Children from divorced homes or who experience extreme turbulence at home are twice as likely to drop out of school as those from intact homes, three times more prone to have a baby out of wedlock, five-fold more likely to be in poverty, and twelve times more apt to be incarcerated. (M. J. McManus, *Ethics & Religion* (2004)).

3. As *Bubbe* (Grandmother) used to say, there are two things that a parent cannot take credit for: how their kids turn out and how their *chulent* turns out. A person can put in all the right ingredients and it still may not turn out as they had hoped. Sometimes God has other plans, despite our best efforts.

---

child though, does not gain self-esteem in the same way that an adult does.

Children gain their self-esteem largely from their parents (or primary caregivers). They do not possess the reasoning faculties to make choices as adults do, and thus cannot gain self-respect through self-control. Our personal sense of right and wrong is not fully established until our early teens.[4] Children are completely egocentric until the age of twelve and thirteen, girls and boys respectively.

You can fall short in every area of parenting, but as long as you give your child self-esteem, he or she will still have a good chance of being a happy, well-adjusted individual. Conversely, if you fail in this one area, you can do everything else by the book and still have a very tough time raising an emotionally healthy child.

How do you instill your child with a feeling of self-worth? You must establish within your child the knowledge that *he or she is the path to your happiness rather than the obstacle to it.*[5]

I was a guest at a Shabbos table a while ago, when the mother, in front of all her children and my own family, began to describe an awful, traumatic experience she had once suffered: a snow day. Apparently she was trapped in this box she calls her house with these little people who look a little like her and her husband, and she couldn't get out. She proceeded to relate in

---

4.   This is the reasoning behind the Torah's view of a boy or girl coming of age once he reaches the age of thirteen or twelve, respectively. The Torah teaches that a child cannot be held completely accountable for his actions in the *Beis Din* (Rabbinical court) until these respective ages.

5.   We are not speaking of making our child responsible for our emotional wellbeing. It is harmful to tell a child that, "It hurts me when you are angry." Rather, the message—both verbal and nonverbal—to communicate is, that when your child is around you, he or she brings you joy.

great detail this awful "waste-of-a-day" experience, stuck in the house all day long with her own children.

Now, while the mother was regaling us with her tale, her children were seated at the table, happily eating their *gefilte* fish, but they most certainly heard their mother's words, internalized them, and were affected by them.

How might a husband feel if he overheard his wife say to her friend, "Oy, it's snowing. Moshe can't get the car out and I'm stuck with him in the house all day; what am I going to do?" Or how would a woman feel returning home after a long day, only to be greeted by her husband in the following way, "You're back so soon! I was hoping for a little peace and quiet. Can you go to a friend's house?" We're adults, yet that would hurt us. How do you imagine a child would feel? The unspoken message children too often receive from their parents is, "I'm happy when you go on the bus, and I'm miserable when you come home. It's not that I don't love you—of course I do—but you make my life difficult."

A child who feels as if he or she is nothing more than an obligation, a person whom their parents grudgingly endure, will not—*cannot*—grow up to feel good about themselves, much less have a healthy relationship with his or her parents.

Your child is always going to equate your feelings towards them with their feelings toward themselves. Egocentric beings (such as children) correlate their self-worth with the way they are treated by others. *If my mother and father think that I am somebody who brings them joy, then I'm worthy, and I can feel good about myself.* Conversely, it is easy for children to ascribe a failure within themselves as the reason behind a parent's behavior. When a parent ignores, or begrudingly endures a child, the child naturally concludes that there is a flaw within herself.

She translates her parent's attitude into the thought that, "I am unworthy of his love," which soon becomes, "I am unworthy of being loved."

If, as children, we did not receive parental love, or felt that our lives were out of control due to trauma or domestic volatility, we may spend the rest of our lives craving love and acceptance.[6]

Praise Versus Criticism

Some parents believe that good parenting means to point out every wrong thing that the child does. Can you guess what the praise to criticism ratio is in most households, the number of times you praise a child versus the number of times you criticize him or her? One to forty. If you think about it, it makes sense. Because once a day you're conscious of good behavior: "Oh, Chaim, very good boy." The rest of the time it's, "Take your shoes off, put your feet down, don't do that, what are you doing, stop hitting him, don't do that, do this, do that . . ." Could you imagine if your boss criticized you forty times during the day, and gave you only a single compliment? It would wear you down.

Be alert of this when dealing with your child, and you will be amazed at how your relationship with your child will improve when he begins to hear streams of praise instead of an avalanche of criticism from his sole source of emotional

---

6.   K. Bolger, C. Patterson, J., and Kupersmidt, "Peer Relationships and Self-esteem Among Children Who Have Been Maltreated," *Child Development*, 69(4), (1998), pp. 1171–1197.

sustenance.[7] Do not underestimate the tremendous power of your loving acceptance (or harsh criticism).

If a child does not receive adequate attention through positive means, he will often try to get noticed in a negative way. Even though his actions are sure to bring an unpleasant and even abusive consequence, so strong is the drive for a relationship and acknowledgement that the child will do almost anything to feel noticed. You cannot give a greater gift to your child than the feeling that he is valuable; and inoculate him from the "I'm not worth much disease" that afflicts so many adults today.[8]

Give Your Child Freedom

We can ask any parent about child-rearing's two most difficult phases. The answer is invariably the "terrible twos" and adolescence. This pattern is easily understood in terms of control and respect. A two-year-old is gaining a sense of independence and wants to exercise this freedom. The teenager also wants to express his individuality. In both scenarios, the parents seek to place limits, and conflict ensues. Both parties lack the power they want and neither feels respected.

---

7. "One should never single out one child from among the others for special treatment, because on account of two *selas'* (a coin) weight of fine wool that Yaakov gave to Yosef more than his other sons, the brothers envied him and this led to the events which caused our forefathers to go down to Egypt" (*Shabbos* 10b). The brothers took this discrepancy as a criticism; thus, a parent should praise all children equally.

8. There was a time when your child brought you unimaginable joy. Your thoughts and very existence revolved around your child and his or her needs and happiness. No detail was too small if it concerned your child's welfare and well-being. This was when your child was first born. Gratitude pervaded into every fiber of your being. When you re-connect with this feeling of gratitude, you will help to produce a suitable state of mind.

One of the most dangerous things to do in raising children (and we use the word *dangerous* because there are significant ramifications) is to impose even greater restrictions as they yearn for self-expression.

We discussed previously that self-control leads to self-respect. Our children must also feel a sense of control in order to exercise this expanded sense of emotional and spiritual freedom, to be able to make decisions and live by the consequences.

When a child at any age moves away from Torah observance, and goes off the *derech*, his parents often try to tighten the noose. This is counter-productive because the more you impose restrictions, the more the child will rebel. The way to help avoid this problem is to allow him to make choices that are age-appropriate and halachically and legally responsible.[9] In this way, he will be far less inclined to defy you. Yes, he's going to make some unappealing decisions. We can live with those. You have to pick your battles; decide what is important and

---

9. One should seek consultation with a Rabbi who represents *da'as Torah* (pure Torah outlook) and who has experience in dealing with children-at-risk in order to set appropriate halachic guidelines. A man is responsible to ensure that his wife, children and members of his household all achieve perfection and freedom from transgression (*Shulchan Aruch, Even HaEzer* 178:21); Rambam, *Hilchos Sotah* 4:19). Even so, this should not result in an atmosphere of excessive fear in the home, since this can cause more harm than good. A man should therefore speak softly and gently even regarding serious transgressions (*Gittin* 6b).

Dealing with rebellious children can be as severe as the war of "Gog and Magog [at the End of Days]" (Cf. *Berachos* 7b). Despite the difficulties, such children can still be brought back to *teshuvah* "through bonds of love" (Chazon Ish, *Yoreh De'ah* 2:16). The Gemara (*Yevamos* 62b) states that through behaving with love and respect one can merit to direct one's children on the straight path. Nowadays, one should not be overly insistent when enforcing rules regarding *ruchnius* (spirituality), but focus instead on matters of *derech eretz* (common decency). If their behavior is likely to negatively affect a sibling, one should tread very carefully and seek the wise counsel of a qualified Rabbi (*Mishpatei Shalom* 9:20).

what is not. If you try to totally control your child now, you can be assured that when you no longer have influence, the child will not only move away from Judaism, but from you as well.

The flip side is that you must ensure that you are striking a balance, and are not being too lax and permissive. Sometimes parents cannot effectively make a child feel loved and instead, they permit activities that are inappropriate. If you give in to your child over everything because you fear alienating him, he will soon realize that you are scared, and will push your limits even further.

Examining our relationship with God sheds light on the importance of balancing independence with submission. In order for us to maximize our potential, human beings need to be autonomous; at the same time this independence mandates that we are submissive to God's will. As with our children, we must help to instill in them a sense of independence while recognizing that they must acquiesce to our will, for their good; otherwise they will not properly cultivate the ability to delay gratification;[10] the vehicle for growth.

---

10. A landmark experiment dubbed, The Marshmallow Test looked into the ability of children to delay gratification. Conducted at Stanford University, researchers gave a marshmallow to a series of children with the following offer: either eat this one marshmallow right away or, if the child was willing to wait a short while, he or she would receive an additional marshmallow. The researcher then left the room, and the child was alone, with marshmallow in hand. Fourteen years later, the researchers tracked down the children and found that those who had been able to delay gratification—and hold out for two marshmallows—had better overall test scores, social skills, and self-esteem than their counterparts. See Y. Shoda, W. Mischel, and P. K. Peake, "Predicting Adolescent Cognitive and Self-regulatory Competencies from Preschool Delay of Gratification: Identifying diagnostic conditions," *Developmental Psychology* 26:6 (1990), p. 978–986.

25

The Adult Child: Help Your Older Child Eliminate Self-Destructive Habits

Whether it is smoking, drinking, or openly leading an unhealthy lifestyle, if you want to help your child kick bad habits and get his life back on track, then you must *daven* (pray), and endeavor to follow the strategies below.[1]

Let us first remind ourselves of the psychology at play, excerpted from my book, *Real Power*:[2]

> To the degree we lack self-esteem our psyche is plagued by desires, fleeting impulses, and urges that twist and pull at our thoughts. When we are alone, in order to quiet the unconscious voice that whispers, "I don't like me," we do whatever we can to feel good and numb the pain. We spiral downward, because a person who has a poor self-image often seeks the temporary,

---

1.   If the child is addicted to drugs or alcohol, or displays signs of psychological disorder, even with the best intentions, parents cannot always solve their children's problems alone, and should therefore seek Rabbinic, and/or psychological help.

2.   D. Lieberman, *Real Power* (Viter Press, 2008) pp. 75–76.

hollow refuge of immediate gratification, and gives in to his impulses instead of rising above them. [3]

When the ego reigns, our emotions cloud our thoughts, and our choices are unproductive and sometimes harmful. When we do not like who we are—which again, is true for all human beings, to varying degrees— we punish ourselves with activities that are disguised as pleasurable: excessive eating, alcohol or drug abuse, and endless, meaningless distractions. We desperately want to *love* ourselves, but instead we *lose* ourselves. Unable to invest in our own wellbeing, we substitute illusions for love. These ethereal pleasures mask our self-contempt, and because the comfort sought is rewarded instead by greater pain, we descend further into despair.[4]

---

3.   In *Mishlei* (1:17), we find the analogy of a bird who sees food in a trap. Although on one level he knows that he will be caught, his desire for food causes him to close his eyes and act as if the trap did not exist. This is what desire does to a person. It causes him to willfully close his eyes to the dangers.

4.   Your goal as a parent is to teach your child to walk and then teach him to walk away—to impart in him a sense of independence. When we seek to rescue our child from every difficulty he encounters, we temporarily ease his burden but cause him to suffer from an unintended consequence—the blurring of the line between behavior and impact. This creates a learned helplessness which under- mines the child's innate desire to effect change in himself and to grow emo- tionally and spiritually. We all should emulate the ants, who are self-sufficient, instead of being sluggards, who are always in crisis (see *Mishlei* 6:6–11). Free will is built on the foundation of personal responsibility. As it is written, "For though the *tzaddik* (righteous person) may fall seven times, he will arise . . ." (*Mishlei* 24:16). In some instances, we need to take a step back so that our child can stand on his own; and should he fall, get back up on his own.

A Two-Hundred-Year-Old Story

A royal prince once went mad and thought he was a turkey. He felt compelled to sit naked under the table, pecking at bones and pieces of bread like a turkey. The royal physicians gave up all hope of curing him of this madness, and the king suffered tremendous grief.

A sage came and said, "I will undertake to cure him."

Then the sage undressed and sat naked under the table next to the prince, pecking at crumbs and bones.

"Who are you?" asked the prince. "What are you doing here?"

"And you?" replied the sage. "What are you doing here?"

"I am a turkey," said the prince.

"I am also a turkey," answered the sage.

They sat together like this for some time, and eventually they became good friends. One day the sage signaled the king's servants to throw him his shirt. He said to the prince, "What makes you think that a turkey can't wear a shirt? You can wear a shirt and still be a turkey." With that, the two of them put on shirts.

After a while, the sage signaled the servants again, and they threw him a pair of pants. Then he said to the prince, "What makes you think you can't be a turkey if you wear pants?" The sage continued in this manner until they were both completely dressed.

Soon he signaled again, and he and the prince were given regular food from the table. Then the sage said, "What makes you think you will stop being a turkey if you eat good food? You can eat whatever you want and still be a turkey!" They both ate the food.

Finally, the sage said, "What makes you think a turkey must sit under a table? Even a turkey can sit at the table, and a turkey can also walk around anyplace it wants and no one objects."

The prince thought this through and accepted the wise man's opinion. Once he got up and walked about like a human being, he also began behaving like one.

This two-hundred-year-old fable illuminates the dynamics involved in the process of change. We will refer to this fable again as we discuss these factors.[5]

Psychological Component 1: Unconditional Love

After the sage in the fable made himself indistinguishable from the prince, he didn't try to convince him of anything. He just spent time with him. A vital ingredient of healing is unconditional love. That means expressing—through words and deeds—"I unconditionally accept you for who you are. Even if you never change, it is okay."[6]

Many people constantly criticize the person they are trying to heal. Then, the unconditional love becomes diluted. It requires tremendous focus, dedication, and patience to

---

5. "The Turkey Prince" is based on an old Chassidic tale authored by the Breslover Rebbe, Rabbi Nachman of Breslov. Attribution to psychological factors was made by Rabbi Aryeh David Nivin.

6. The concept of unconditional love becomes more complicated where, in extremely rare cases, a person's behavior classifies him as "wicked," requiring us to follow a different procedure. Dealing with such circumstances requires careful direction from a qualified Rabbi, and is beyond the scope of this work.

continually accept someone in the face of difficult behavior. Yet this is precisely what the sage did.

Avoid the urge to judge. Be mindful that no one will change unless he likes who he is.[7] Your child gains a sense of ephemeral worth from others, and your child must feel acceptance from you in order to feel good about himself; and as he begins to care about himself, self-destructive behaviors lose their luster.

Psychological Component 2: Consistency and Joy

It is important to maintain a positive attitude. Smile when you are together and let your positivity come through. Offer to do things together to show your child that you enjoy being with him and that you're not simply hanging around to check up on him. You don't want your child to feel that he is a burden, or as if he is your project; and that you are being nice because it's a mitzvah or in order to ease your guilt. Rather, convey that you are making an incredible effort because he enhances your life and you want to be a part of his.

Psychological Component 3: One Thing at a Time, and One Thing Only

Do not overwhelm the person you are trying to help. We saw in the turkey fable that there were at least five stages of healing: wearing the shirt, wearing the pants, being completely dressed, eating regular food, and then sitting at the table. Sometimes we make the mistake of trying to impart too much, too fast,

---

7. A person acts in accordance with how he sees himself. The Sages therefore teach, "Do not judge yourself to be a wicked person" (*Pirkei Avos* 2:18); "Do not consider yourself inferior" (*Pirkei Avos* 2:13).

and when things are going well, there is a temptation to speed up the process. Be careful of this or your child can burn out. As long as there is movement in a constructive direction, you will have momentum on your side, and his success in these areas will give him the confidence to make further changes.

Psychological Component 4: Begin With an Instant Success

Why did the sage choose to have the prince put on a shirt first? After all, it's far worse to be without pants than without a shirt. The wise man understood a profound principle (discussed in more detail in Chapter 17): when trying to change someone, begin with the easiest and most potentially successful step, something that will make the person feel good about himself— and then move on from there.

If a parent wants to stop his child from drinking all night and sleeping all day, he must focus on a smaller issue first: for instance, the condition of the child's apartment. At first, he will simply keep dishes from piling up in the sink, then progress to keeping clothes off the floor, and so on. While these might seem like inanely small steps, to the person who doesn't care about himself or what he does, these actions are literally life-changing.[8]

---

8. "If someone is not used to being involved in matters of major importance, even minor matters take on great importance in his eyes . . . An example of this is making purchases. To a poor person every small item he buys is a major event and he is careful about each penny. But to the president of a large corporation only business deals involving large sums of money are important." (*Chochmah u'Mussar*, vol. 1, p. 317).

Psychological Component 5: Stability Within Structure

When we create structure in our lives, we allow for growth; otherwise our energy dissipates. Structure helps us to move in a meaningful, productive direction, while preventing us from succumbing to passing whims and desires. Lack of structure does not free us; it paralyzes us. Aptly, the Hebrew prayer book is called the *siddur,* which means "order."[9]

Help your child to build a structure around healthy values that he aspires to embrace, thus creating a stable framework upon which the days' events can hang.

Psychological Component 6: A New You in a New Land

The philosopher Friedrich Nietzsche once mused, "Insanity in individuals is something rare, but in groups, parties, nations, and epochs, it is the rule." An illustration is the mob mentality, the phenomenon where people in groups tend to support more extreme ideas than they would on an individual basis.

Municipalities, too, are aware that graffiti needs to be removed as quickly as possible, because as soon as it appears, it creates a breeding ground for vandalism perpetrated by others who previously thought it unacceptable.

The influence of our surroundings has been demonstrated by extensive research.[10] As well, the Torah instructs us that our

---

9. "One who learns without structure cannot acquire wisdom. His learning is mixed up in his mind, and nothing is retained with clarity" (Ramchal, *Sefer HaVikuach,* p. 76).

10. J. Joseph, "Is Crime in the Genes? A Critical Review of Twin and Adoption Studies of Criminality and Antisocial Behavior," *The Journal of Mind and Behavior,*

character is greatly influenced by our environment.[11] This is the lesson of the following excerpt from *Pirkei Avos*:

> Rabbi Yossi ben Kisma said: One time I was walking along the way and a certain man met me. He greeted me and I returned the greeting. He said to me, "Rabbi, where are you from?" I responded, "I am from a great city of scholars and scribes." He said, "Rabbi, would you be willing to dwell among us in our place, and I will give you thousands of thousands of gold coins, precious stones, and pearls?" I replied: "Even if you would give me all the silver, gold, precious stones, and pearls in the world, I would not dwell anywhere other than a place of Torah."[12]

Parenthetically, the converse is also true, which explains why a person may act totally out of character while on vacation or otherwise visiting another city. We are, in part, a product of our surroundings, and the pull from the environment—both positive and negative—is strong.

Our identity is very much tied in with where we live, the people we know, and the places we go.[13] By removing individuals from their environment, you shake up their self-concepts and make it easier for them to envision themselves differently. You also get them away from the influences that keep them

---

22 (2001), pp. 179–218.

11.   "Fortunate is he who does not walk in the council of the wicked or sit in a place of scoffers" (*Tehillim* 1:1). "Woe unto the wicked, and woe unto his neighbor; it is good for the *tzaddik* [righteous person] and it is good for his neighbor" (*Sukkah* 56b).

12.   *Pirkei Avos* 6:9.

13.   "A person is drawn after the society he lives in" (Rambam, *Hilchos De'os* 6:1).

locked into negative patterns. In some instances, then, you may want to encourage the child to distance himself from unconducive surroundings.[14]

Psychological Component 7: Great Expectations

It's no secret that we tend to live up to what is expected of us. Marketers know it. Politicians know it. Teachers know it. Parents know it.

The Law of Expectancy predicts that when a person expects us to achieve a certain outcome, we often rise to meet that expectation.

This principle is beautifully illustrated in a true story about a troublesome class in one of the worst school districts in New Jersey. The kids in this class continually scored Cs, Ds, and Fs. They were every teacher's worst nightmare—a disruptive, unmanageable bunch for whom, you had to figure, Juvenile Detention was surely just a prank or two away.

But one day, a new teacher arrived and took over this unruly class. Within a single semester, the students' grades improved a notch—from Cs, Ds, and Fs to Bs, Cs, and Ds. By the second semester, the entire class had an overall B-minus average, a level of achievement that was unprecedented for this class.

The school district honored this teacher with a Teacher of the Year award. "What's your secret?" the superintendent asked her. "You turned an unruly mob of kids that everyone had given

---

14. The depth of the issues and the leverage that you have will determine the optimum way to accomplish this; and we are not speaking of shipping our children off to fend for themselves without any emotional support. Rather, a change in schools, a summer program in another city or country, and the like. In some instances, a short break of a few weeks or so, is enough to gain a foothold in their attitude; sometimes a more permanent move might be required.

up on into scholars! They show up for class every day, they're engaged, they want to learn, get good grades, be better citizens. How did you do it?"

"Oh, it wasn't so hard," the teacher replied. "I could see their potential. I saw their IQ scores the first day of class."

The superintendent seemed puzzled. "But these kids all have below-average IQs . . ." he said.

"No," the teacher shook her head, "look here . . ." She whipped out a paper and handed it to him. "125, 130, 140, 118 . . ."

The superintendent smiled. "Ma'am, those aren't IQ scores. Those are their locker numbers."

Sometimes the faith of one dedicated teacher, however mistaken its roots, can work miracles.

This hopeful teacher never talked down to her kids, never treated them as if they were "less than." She never said: "That's a silly question!" as so many other teachers before her had done. She greeted every question with: "What a great question! Only smart people ask those kinds of questions!" Every day she taught them new things, never wavering in her belief that they could learn and ultimately achieve. Confidence is contagious.

Nearly every single thing we're told about ourselves, certainly when we're young and impressionable—and especially from a teacher or parent—we take as unbiased truth. If a teacher tells you that you're dumb, guess what? You believe you're dumb. But if a teacher says, "That's a smart question!" you believe you're smart, you believe in your own potential, and you *act* smarter and try harder.

But it goes further. Researchers sought to discover if, perhaps, the impact of expectancy could have an even more far-reaching and powerful effect—does a child actually *become* brighter? This is what psychologists wondered when they launched a well-known study to test this very hypothesis.[15]

A group of children was administered a nonverbal test of intelligence, which was disguised as a test that would predict intellectual blooming. The test was labeled, "The Harvard Test of Inflected Acquisition."

There were eighteen classrooms in the school, three at each of the six grade levels. Within each grade level, the three classrooms were comprised of children with above-average ability, average ability, and below-average ability. Approximately 20 percent of the children in each of the eighteen classrooms were chosen randomly to form the experimental group. The teachers of these children were told that the children's scores on the "Test of Inflected Acquisition" indicated that they would show surprising gains in intellectual competence during the next eight months of school.

In actuality, the only difference between the experimental group and the control group children, then, was the belief of the teachers. Eight months later, all the children were retested, using the same intelligence test. Overall, the children for whom the teachers had been led to expect greater intellectual gain showed *a significantly greater gain over the children in the control group*— their IQs went up an average of 20 points. The children didn't just do better, they *became smarter*.

The research literature on interpersonal expectancy effects has expanded to include 345 experiments in eight separate domains of research—all demonstrating a clear-cut correlation between expectation and actual performance, and enhanced aptitude.

---

15.   R. Rosenthal and L. Jacobson, *Pygmalion in the Classroom* (NY: Holt, Rinehart & Winston, 1968).

Expectancy is a double-edged sword: we also tend to live up to someone's *negative* expectations of us, and our own negative expectations for ourselves. Put another way, we tend to rise only to the level of excellence that we—and others—believe we will.

What message are you conveying to your child? Does he believe that *you* believe in him?

A Simple Test

There is a legendary businessman, who, in his autobiography, revealed that he had always assumed that he was very intelligent. After retiring, he took an IQ test only to learn that he was at the lower end of average. He wrote that had he found this out when he was a young man, he never would have achieved a fraction of his success.[16] In fact, research shows us that there are different types of intelligence and learning styles. Consequently, a child who does poorly on a standardized learning test and can't sit still in a classroom may very well be a genius and capable of learning material at a pace that is far beyond his classmates—but instead, he is labeled as having learning or behavioral difficulties.

---

16.   D. Ogilvy, *Ogilvy on Advertising* (John Wiley and Sons, 1983).

Techniques to Maximize the Parent and Adult-Child Relationship

The stress that can be caused due to conflict between parents and their adult children is immense. Much of this tension, however, can be alleviated by the application of some simple strategies. There are four major areas of contention that can occur between a parent and adult child:

Hot Button # 1: Input and Advice

Parent's Perspective

Your adult children need and crave your emotional support and acceptance, but there's one thing they don't want: advice. As well-meaning and well-intentioned as you are, they don't want to hear it, they often resent it, and you accordingly must limit it.[1]

Once, after giving a talk, an elderly gentleman came up to me and said, "I'm having a problem with one of my children—

---

1. This does not apply when the child invites, welcomes, or encourages a parent's input.

he doesn't take my advice and we get into an argument every time I try to tell him that he's making a mistake."

I said, "Then stop giving advice."

"I can't do that," he answered instantly.

"Why not?" I inquired.

He said, "Well, he does too many foolish things, and has these silly ideas and plans that never work out."

I probed further. "Does he ever take your advice?"

"No," he said.

"How many years has this been going on?" I asked.

"Oh, I'd say about fifty years or so," he said with a laugh. Recognizing that my window to help him was narrow and closing, I was blunt, "So, what is it that you're hoping to accomplish other than continuing to harm the relationship?"

There was a long pause, a faint smile, and then an honest, "I don't know." I encouraged him to experiment with the idea of not giving advice for a 30-day period, and then see what happens. "At the very least," I said, "your relationship will improve."

Let's be aware of the deeper psychology here: When you constantly thrust advice onto an adult child, particularly one who has low self-esteem, and that's all of us to some degree, what is the unconscious message that you're communicating? *I don't trust your judgment.* It should come as no surprise that such input is going to cause the child to push back, and move further away.[2]

In a situation where you feel that your child is not thinking clearly, be shrewd in your approach. For instance, in a casual,

---

2.   It is for this reason that it is sometimes advisable not to go into business with family members; giving suggestions, input, and even orders are necessary to the smooth running of any company, but such a level of interaction can be damaging to the personal relationship.

non-confrontational way, ask him if he has fully considered all the options—"I'm sure you've looked into this very well, I was just wondering what you think of . . ." —then drop it!

As a result, your child will be more inclined to consider your input, because it's not coming from a position of "I'm older, I have more experience than you."

You will also find that if you are able to communicate and demonstrate to your child how much you love and respect him, and how proud you are of him, then he won't feel the need to dig in his emotional heels when you offer advice. Instead, he'll be able to hear your counsel as it is intended, and not become instinctively defensive.

Child's Perspective

When listening to unwanted advice given by parents or in-laws, you can still pay attention to them without necessarily agreeing with them. Furthermore, it won't hurt you to take their advice every once in a while. You should remember that there's no mitzvah in the Torah that says you have to be right, but there is a mitzvah to honor your parents, and in-laws.[3]

---

3   A person is also required to honor his parents-in-law, as they are considered like parents. King David addressed King Saul as "father" since he was his father-in-law. (*Shulchan Aruch, Yoreh De'ah* 240:24; *Taz*, ad loc. #19).

Regarding just listening to one's parents, even if one disagrees with them: It is a Torah mitzvah to honor and respect one's parents (*Shemos* 20:12; *Vayikra* 19:3). Thus, a child is not permitted to deny the validity of his or her parents' words or to contradict them. (*Shulchan Aruch, Yoreh De'ah* 240:2) However, it is permitted to disagree in matters of *halachah* and Torah learning (*Pischei Teshuvah,* ad loc. #1).

Hot Button # 2: Boundaries

Parent's Perspective

Parents of adult children must learn to respect boundaries. Unless it is accepted and appreciated protocol, rule number one is to call before coming over. In fact, call before you call . . . what does this mean? When you phone, don't assume that your child is relaxing with a glass of iced tea flipping through the newspaper, waiting for the phone to ring. When you call, it really goes a long way to ask if now is a good time for your child to speak.

When your child or child-in-law knows that he can exit the conversation quickly, without feeling guilty, he'll pick up the phone more often, rather than looking at caller ID, thinking to himself that he doesn't have the time or energy right now to speak to you.

Certainly, when you get the dreaded "machine," do not leave a guilt-inducing phone message: "Okay, I see you're not home, I'm assuming you're not home—why else wouldn't you pick up? I just happen to have gone by your house earlier, and I saw all four cars in the driveway. Maybe you're having a party, I don't know. OK . . . it's me . . . are you there? I haven't heard from you in awhile . . ."

While the obligation of respect falls more squarely on the child than the parent, when the parent gives due respect, the child is far more likely to reciprocate.[4]

---

4   In this vein, a parent should not impose excessive burdens on his children or demand honor from them, for these things will eventually cause his children to violate their obligations of honor and respect. A parent should forgive slights and ignore infractions, since a parent is allowed to yield his honor. (*Shulchan Aruch, Yoreh De'ah* 240:19), quoted in Rabbi Ehrman, *Journey to Virtue* (Artscroll), 44:27).

Child's Perspective

A boundary issue is clear when the child's marriage is negatively affected by irresponsible behavior by a parent or in-law.[5]

If you find that your parents' or in-laws' frequent calls and visits are overwhelming, consider that their intention is not to impose, but rather to have a relationship with you, and to be a part of your lives.

Rather than allowing the tension to build up, there is nothing wrong with establishing boundaries, as long as you speak respectfully and lovingly to your parents. When you express your feelings, make sure you convey how important the relationship is to you, and how you want to improve and strengthen the quality of communication between you.

Hot Button # 3: Money and Support

Parent's Perspective

To parents who provide their adult child with financial support, if you are offering money for a specific reason, it is perfectly reasonable to say: "We want to give you money for XYZ—to lease this car, to go to Israel, to get a tutor, and so on." Your child can either accept or reject your offer.

However, for the adult parent who is financially supporting a child, either partially or entirely, *give the money unconditionally*. If there are strings attached, you're using the money as a weapon that will only serve to damage the relationship.

---

5   The Torah gives a firm directive to establish boundaries. "A man shall leave his father and mother and cleave to his wife; and they shall become one flesh" (*Bereishis* 2:24).

It is likely that any parent who uses money to control his adult child now has tried every other way to control him when he was younger, to no avail.

If your child is relying on you for financial support, he is probably already feeling a sense of dependency and perhaps even inadequacy. And now you're going to control how he spends the money and lives his life? Nobody wins. Parents who use money as a way of exerting influence over their child's life should be aware that such an attitude could result in alienation and ultimately estrangement.

Now you may be thinking: *It's my money, I worked hard for it, and I'm not going to let my child waste it away. I have the right to tell my child how I want him to spend it.* The answer is that yes, it is your money, but if you choose to give it to your child, then give it unconditionally, or not at all.

No one gives a gift, a shirt, for example, and then demand that the recipient wear it only on Tuesdays. Give the money without conditions.

Child's Perspective

If you are being supported by a parent or in-law, you must decide whether accepting parental assistance is worthwhile. Often, money will solve one problem, while creating many others; and sometimes it's not worth the exchange rate—you're giving up too much.

Nonetheless, you'll find an amazing thing happens when you respectfully tell your parent or parent-in-law, "We very much appreciate your desire to help us and we love you for it. But this is not the way we want to live our lives, and so we can't accept the money under these conditions." The response just may be, "Good. Let's talk about it."

There's a saying in negotiation: He who wants it less, wins. You have to be able to look at a situation and say, "Is this worth it?", and be willing to walk away from the table if you decide it's not.

Hot Button # 4: Mixed Emotions

Parent's Perspective

Often, parents disapprove of their children's life decisions and while you may have hoped and prayed that your child would turn out differently, you have to let it go.

If your child feels that he is a disappointment as a result of the message of disapproval you have either verbally or non-verbally communicated, there will be dejection on both sides. Although he may not be leading the life you wanted for him in the way you intended, you still may, and should choose, from this point in time on, to love your child unconditionally.

You always have the opportunity to tell your child how much you care about him, how much you love him, how much you respect him, and how proud you are of him. If you think it won't make a difference because you're 90 and he's 70, you're wrong. It matters.

Child's Perspective

Your parent's disapproval can cause immeasurable hurt, and even cause you to question your self-worth. As an adult child, though, remind yourself that your parent only desires your happiness, even though this wish can often manifest itself in curious, and even contradictory, ways.

If you were mistreated as a child, and did not receive adequate love and attention, chances are you are walking around with a great deal of anger and pain.

However, despite the legacy of self-loathing as a result of a difficult childhood, you can transform the way you see yourself, and your relationship when you embrace the following truism: *The love that parents give children is determined by their own limitations, not those of the children. A person who doesn't love himself cannot give love. All he can do is control and take.*

Our feelings of self-worth are often tied to the way people relate to us, but this is an erroneous conclusion. As adults, it can still be difficult to appreciate that our self-worth is not contingent upon our parents' acceptance of us, but we can recreate this emotional imprint. Once we do, our lives can be forever changed, and the damage that has disfigured us for decades can be undone.

If you see a person in a wheelchair, you wouldn't get mad at that person because he can't get out and walk. Somebody who is emotionally handicapped is equally challenged. Does it make sense to resent a parent for not being able to give to you something that he or she doesn't have? Do you want to hold onto anger because your mother or father was, and still may be, incapable of expressing love for you?

Still, you can go one step further. If you show your parent the utmost respect, attention, and kindness—regardless of how you were treated—you enter into a new realm of emotional independence and infuse yourself with a steady stream of self-esteem.

FAQs

Q Is there any point attempting to make peace when the other party doesn't seem to want to try?

A Hope exists for even the most intractable situation, and you'll never know unless you try;[1] so it is your obligation to attempt reconciliation. Think for a moment why you hesitate to try. You fear you might look foolish, waste your time, be embarrassed, you've already given so much, and so forth. All of these concerns are tied into the ego.

The Sage, the *Pele Yoetz*, suggests that as an incentive for doing something that could potentially be uncomfortable, we should focus on the reward we receive for making peace. He provides a striking example. Imagine a person approaches you and asks you to make peace with someone you can't stand. Your initial reaction is to immediately turn down the offer. Then the person asks, "What if I give you fifty dollars? Do you think you could try? How about a hundred dollars? Or a thousand dollars? If I give you a hundred thousand dollars, could you do it? How about two million dollars?" There is a point at which every person would give in and decide it is worth the effort to make peace.

---

1. Even if there is no immediate expectation of peace, one should still make every possible effort, in the hope that he will eventually succeed, like we find by Moshe Rabbeinu and Korach. (See *Bamidbar* 16:2 and Rashi, ad loc.).

According to the *Pele Yoetz*, the reward we get in *Olam Haba* (the World to Come) for making peace far outweighs any financial bonus this world can offer. By reminding ourselves that a small act now will reap an eternity of benefit, it is easier to make the right decisions.[2]

There is another reason why you should try to make peace. After decades of estrangement, Yaakov finally made peace with his brother Eisav. Afterwards, the Torah states, "Yaakov arrived whole (*shalem*) to the city of Shechem."[3] The word for peace, *shalom*, derives from the word *shalem*, which means whole. Our willingness to do what is necessary to bring peace is what will ultimately give us peace (to the degree that God allows), *regardless* of the outcome.[4]

Q How many times should I attempt to make peace, and for how long should I try?

A If, over a period of time, after several attempts at reconciliation (the halachah stipulates that three attempts should be made)[5] you continue to meet with

---

2.   *Pele Yoetz*, entries "Sechar Mitzvah," and "Machlokes."

3.   *Bereishis* 33:18.

4.   One way to understand why God sets such a value on peace is because it negates the illusion that we are distinct from others, and that all of us are separate from Him. The ego divides, and this is the cause of conflict. Peace wipes away the misperception of multiplicity and reinforces the pervading unity of our reality.

5.   The Rambam (*Hilchos Teshuvah* 2:9) states that if a person is not appeased, the sinner must bring three of the injured party's friends and request forgiveness. If he refuses to accept the apology, he does so a second and third time; after which he may cease his attempts. The *Shulchan Aruch* (*Orach Chaim* 606:1) also states that if the person is not appeased the first time he must return a second and third time—each time with three friends. If the person refused to be appeased, the sinner is exempt thereafter. The *Magen Avraham* (ad loc.) adds that he should try to appease the injured in a different way each time. He may also make more

great resistance, then it might be best to move on. The quality of any relationship is determined by the one who wants it least, not most. But there is a difference between someone not *wanting* to forgive and someone who is *uninterested* in having any type of relationship. If the other person—or both people, if you are acting as a third party—has no interest in reconciling, perhaps it is best to let things be.

If it's a case, however, where the hurt is too intense for this person to move past it now, revisit the situation after a few months or a year, depending on what happened, and try again. Because in this instance, it is the freshness of the pain, rather than a lack of desire to reconcile, that is impeding reconciliation.[6]

Q I don't want anything to do with this person. Is it still necessary to forgive?

A Forgiveness allows us to let go of the past and helps us to move forward. This is a function of human design, whereby we hold on to painful experiences (physical as well as psychological) in order to learn from those experiences and to avoid repeating them. Until we acknowledge them, they remain part of us. Think of those experiences in our lives that we refuse to release, and contrast them with those we have accepted.

---

than the minimum attempts of appeasement, as long it will not bring disgrace to the Torah. All opinions agree that if a person offended his Rabbi he must ask forgiveness as many times as necessary until the Rabbi is appeased.

6.   It is acceptable to allow the anger to subside on its own. However, if it doesn't, then reconciliation is necessary, as stated by the oft cited verse: "Do not hate your brother in your heart; do not take revenge and do not bear a grudge" (*Vayikra* 19:17). If the offender does not initiate a conciliatory dialogue, then the offended party should be the one to open the dialogue. (Ramban on the Torah, ad loc.).

The essence of idolatry is the belief that God is not the only power influencing life. Anger assumes the same belief. "If one breaks dishes in his anger, it is as if he were involved in idol worship."[7] If you do not forgive, then you do not recognize the true Source of the circumstance.[8] And while you may want nothing to do with this person, anger is not a response that will allow you to deal with him, the situation, and yourself with clarity and objectivity.

When we hold onto anger, we are the ones who suffer— emotionally, spiritually, and physically.[9]

---

7. *Shabbos* 105b.

8. According to the *Sefer HaChinuch* (*Mitzvah* 241, "Do not take revenge"), a person who causes harm to another is merely an agent carrying out the will of God: "At the root of the Mitzvah [lies the purpose] that a person should know and reflect that whatever happens to him, good or bad, is made to happen to him by God, blessed be He. There can be nothing [i.e., no effect] from a human hand, from a man's brother's hand, contrary to the will of God, blessed be He. Therefore, if someone inflicts suffering or pain upon him, he should know in his heart that his evil deeds were the cause, and that God, blessed be He, decreed this upon him. Therefore, one should not plan to take revenge from that person, for he is not the [primary] cause of his trouble; it is transgression that is the cause."

9. Research shows forgiveness to be positively associated with five measures of health: physical symptoms, medications used, sleep quality, fatigue, and somatic complaints. See K. A. Lawler, J. W. Younger, R. L. Piferi, E. Billington, R. Jobe, K. Edmondson, and W. H. Jones, "A Change of Heart: Cardiovascular Correlates of Forgiveness in Response to Interpersonal Conflict," *Journal of Behavioral Medicine* (October 2003).

Afterword

We are not always able to control who comes in and out of our lives, but by adopting strategies that are designed to foster understanding and enhanced communication, you will find yourself in a stronger position to make your relationships as rewarding as possible.

Relationships are the cornerstone of our lives; indeed, almost every major Jewish prayer resonates with a request for peace, illuminating God's love for unity and harmony.[1] The Zohar tells us, that "The name of God is peace, and all is bound together in peace."[2] We are further taught that, "There is a future for the man of peace."[3]

Some of our relationships are effortless, some require more work, and others seem like nothing but work; and while certain conflicts appear to be beyond repair, don't despair. With God's help and perseverance, you can help create the right conditions for forgiveness and reconciliation. Even if you're not successful, only good will come from your sincere efforts to make peace.

We should never lose sight, though, that throughout our days, we must strive to work on ourselves as well as our

---

1. Such prayers include the *Amidah* (Standing Silent Prayer), *Kaddish*, *Birkas HaKohanim* (Priestly Blessing), and *Birkas HaMazon* (Grace After Meals).

2. *Zohar, Vayikra* 10b.

3. *Tehillim* 37:37.

relationships. Recall that the process of growth begins with exercising self-control, which leads to self-esteem, which reduces the ego and continues to widen our perspective; and it is our perspective that determines how we see and respond to the world—the clearer our perspective, the more reality we let in, and the more objective and rational our attitudes, thoughts, and behaviors. We evolve then, into more complete vessels to pursue peace and maintain the healthiest possible relationships.

Books of the Bible

Bereishis	=	Genesis
Shemos	=	Exodus
Vayikra	=	Leviticus
Bamidbar	=	Numbers
Devarim	=	Deuteronomy
Koheles	=	Ecclesiastes
Mishlei	=	Proverbs
Shmuel	=	Samuel

Key to Biblical Names

Aharon	=	Aaron
Asher	=	Asher
Avraham	=	Abraham
Avram	=	Abram
Balak	=	Balak
Billam	=	Bilaam
Devorah	=	Deborah
Dovid	=	David
Eisav	=	Esau
Hevel	=	Abel
Iyov	=	Job
Kayin	=	Cain
Korach	=	Korah
Magog	=	Magog
Mordechai	=	Mordechai
Rivka	=	Rebecca
Serach	=	Serah
Shaul	=	Saul
Shechem	=	Shechem
Shlomo	=	Solomon
Shmuel	=	Samuel
Yehudah	=	Judah
Yisrael	=	Israel
Yitzchak	=	Isaac
Yosef	=	Joseph

Glossary

Baalei Mussar – see "*Mussar*"

Be'er Mayim Chaim – the Chafetz Chaim's copious and in-depth footnotes to the main text of *Sefer Chafetz Chaim*.

Breslov, Rabbi Nachman of (1772–1810) – Breslover Rebbe, born in the Ukrainian village of Medziboz, and passed away 38 years later, in the town of Uman. He was a great-grandson of the Baal Shem Tov.

Breslover Rebbe – see Breslov, Rabbi Nachman of

Broida, Rabbi Simcha Zissel Ziv (1824–1898) – one of the foremost students of Rabbi Yisrael Salanter and a primary figure in the *Mussar* movement. Rabbi Broida was the founder and dean of the Talmud Torah in Kelm, and is often referred to as the *Alter* (Elder) of Kelm. Many of Rabbi Broida's letters to his students were published in a two-volume work, *Chochmah u'Mussar*, Rabbi Yerucham Levovitz and Rabbi Simcha Zissel Halevi Levovitz, eds.

Chafetz Chaim – Rabbi Yisrael Meir HaKohen Kagan (1838–1933). Authored the *Mishnah Berurah*, and the *Sefer Chafetz Chaim*, (among other works), a treatise on the laws governing permitted and prohibited speech. His rulings are generally accepted as binding.

Chasman, Rabbi Leib (1869–1935) – Rabbi in Lithuania and *Mashgiach* of the Chevron Yeshivah. His lectures were printed under the title, *Ohr Yahel*.

Chayei Adam – halachic work written by Rabbi Avraham Danzig (1748–1820) concerning the laws of daily conduct, prayer, Sabbath and holidays—the laws discussed in the *Orach Chaim* section of the *Shulchan Aruch*.

Chazal – an acronym for *Chachameinu zichronam livrachah* – Our Sages of blessed memory. Refers exclusively to the Rabbis of the *Mishnah* and Talmud, and represents the authoritative opinion of the Talmud.

chessed – kindness towards others

Chochmah u'Mussar – see Broida, Rabbi Simcha Zissel Ziv.

Choshen Mishpat – section of *Shulchan Aruch* dedicated to the laws of torts, legal procedure, loans, interest and finance

chulent – the traditional Jewish stew-like dish kept hot in a permissible way and served for the second Shabbos meal. Generally consists of any combination of potatoes, meat, beans, and barley.

da'as Torah – supernal wisdom and clarity attained by only the greatest Torah sages of each generation.

Dessler, Rabbi Eliyahu E. (1891–1954) – A leading figure in the *Mussar* movement, who also incorporated Kabbalistic and Chassidic disciplines into his approach to *avodas Hashem* (Divine service). In the early 1940s, he became the first dean of the Gateshead Kollel in England. Later, he assumed the position of *Mashgiach* of the Ponevezh Yeshiva in Bnei Brak. Rabbi Dessler's essays and letters were published posthumously, under the title *Michtav m'Eliyahu*, selections of which have been published in English under the title, *Strive for Truth*.

halachah, halachos – Torah law(s) in general, or a specific detail(s) of Torah law

Kaddish – Song of praise sanctifying Hashem's Name, written in Aramaic. Recited at set points during prayer, and by mourners for the merit of the deceased. Due to its sanctity, it may only be recited with a *minyan* (a quorum of ten adult Jewish males).

lashon hara – forbidden speech; includes disparaging, slanderous, or harmful statements made about others.

Levovitz, Rabbi Yerucham (1875–1936) – One of the most influential thinkers in the *Mussar* movement of his time. He studied in Slabodka under R. Nosson Tzvi Finkel; then under the *Alter* of Kelm, Rabbi Simcha Zissel Ziv. Rabbi Levovitz was best known as the *Mashgiach* of the Mirrer Yeshivah. His writings were published under the title, *Da'as Chochmah u'Mussar*. His novella on *Chumash* were published under the title, *Da'as Torah*.

Likkutei Moharan – see Rabbi Nachman of Breslov

Luzzato, Rabbi Moshe Chaim (1707–1746) – also known as the Ramchal, an acronym of his initials, is best known for his classic work on piety, *Mesilas Yesharim (Path of the Just)*.

Mesilas Yesharim – "*Path of the Just.*" Rabbi Moshe Chaim Luzzato's classic work on piety. Enumerates a step-by-step program for reaching spiritual greatness.

Michtav m'Eliyahu – see Dessler, Rabbi Eliyahu E.

Mishlei – Book of Proverbs, written by King Solomon with *Ruach HaKodesh* (Divine Spirit).

Mishnah Berurah – the glosses of Rabbi Yisrael Meir HaKohen Kagan (d. 1933 CE) on the first section of the *Shulchan Aruch*, *Orach Chaim*. His rulings are generally accepted as binding.

Mishpatei Shalom – Book dealing with the laws of interpersonal relationships, written by Rabbi Yitzchak Silber.

mitzvah – Any one of the 613 commandments of the Torah; used also to mean any thought, word, or deed that Hashem expects or desires a person to do.

Mussar – The practice of personality development (through exercising moral discipline) within the Jewish tradition, the end goal being perfection of character, cultivation of morality, and emulation of Divine qualities. The Rabbis and teachings associated with this discipline are referred to generally as the *"Baalei Mussar."*

Nedarim – Tractate of the Talmud dealing chiefly with the laws of vows.

Orach Chaim – The first section of the *Shulchan Aruch*. Details the laws pertaining to the schedule of daily Jewish living and the yearly cycle of holidays.

Orchos Tzaddikim – "Ways of the Righteous," an anonymous compendium on key topics in character refinement and piety, first printed in Prague, 1581.

Pele Yoetz – Lit. "Marvelous Counsel," the classic book of guidance and rebuke written by Rabbi Eliezer Papo (c. 1785–1827), Rabbi of Selestria, Bulgaria until his death. Selected portions were translated and published as *The Essential Pele Yoetz: an encyclopedia of ethical Jewish living* (1991), by Rabbi Marc D. Angel.

Pirkei Avos – "*Chapters of our Fathers*," A Tractate of the *Mishnah* concerning improving character and piety

Pirkei d'Rebbi Eliezer – "The Chapters of Rabbi Eliezer," a collection of *Midrashim* and *Aggados* attributed to the 1st Century *Tanna*, Rebbi Eliezer ben Hyrkanus.

Rambam (1134–1204) – Rabbi Moshe ben Maimon, also known as Maimonides. The Rambam is one of the most well-known Torah authorities of all time. His most famous work is his *Mishnah Torah* (Review of the Torah) in which he codified the entire body of Jewish law. This was the product of ten years of work and was one of the first systematic codifications of Jewish law ever written.

Ramban – Rabbi Moshe ben Nachman, also known as Nachmanides. He was born in Spain in 1194, and was the foremost halachist and *kabbalist* of his age. He died in 1270 in Eretz Yisrael.

Rav – A duly ordained Rabbi, qualified to issue a ruling in that particular area of Jewish law.

Rema – Rabbi Moshe Isserles (1530–1572). Author of the *Mapah* (Tablecloth), glosses representative of the Ashkenazic halachic opinion to Rabbi Yosef Karo's *Shulchan Aruch*.

Sefer Chafetz Chaim – see Chafetz Chaim

Sefer Chassidim – "Book of the Pious." A halachic work written by Rabbeinu Yehudah HaChassid, one of the great *Baalei Tosafos* of the 12th century.

Sefer HaChinuch – "The Book of Education." An anonymous work by "a Levite from Barcelona" authored in the 13th Century, first printed in 1523. It is a concise compendium of the 613 *mitzvos* of the Torah, their scope and meaning, in the order they appear in the Torah.

Sefer HaMitzvos – "Book of Commandments." The Rambam's accounting and description of the 613 *mitzvos* of the Torah. Written originally in Arabic, it was translated into Hebrew by Rabbi Moshe ibn Tibbon. The Hebrew translation was first published in 1497. This work is regarded as the most authoritative listing of the commandments, and numerous later works rely on its enumeration (some with minor variations). Other works bear the same name, but *Sefer HaMitzvos* without a qualifier refers to the Rambam's work.

Sefer HaVikuach – "The Book of the Dispute." An account of the proceedings of the Ramban's debate against the Jewish apostate Pablo Christiani. This work was deemed blasphemous by the Dominicans and burned. It also precipitated the Ramban's exile from Spain.

Sefer Mitzvos Katan – a book by Rabbi Yitzchak ben Yosef of Cor-
beil (13th Century France, d. 1280). It is partly an abridg-
ment of *Sefer Mitzvos HaGadol* (*Semag*), listing only those
mitzvos that can be fulfilled in the absence of the Beis
HaMikdash. It was first published in 1277.

Seforno – Rabbi Ovadiah ben Yaakov Seforno (c. 1475–1550)
of Italy, well-known for his commentary on the Torah.

Sha'arei Teshuvah – "*Gates of Repentance*," the classic book on repentance written by Rabbeinu Yona of Gerundi (1210–1263),
first published in 1505.

Shabbos – the Sabbath, the Jewish day of rest

shalom – peace, harmony

shalom bayis – marital harmony, also family harmony

She'elos u'Teshuvos Tzitz Eliezer – the 22 volume halachic responsa
of Rabbi Eliezer Yehudah Waldenberg (1915–2006), a leading *posek* of the 20th Century.

Shelah HaKadosh – Rabbi Yeshaya Halevi Horowitz (c. 1565–
1630), called "the Holy *Shelah*," an acronym of his most famous
book, *Shnei Luchos Habris*, "Two Tablets of the Covenant," first
published in 1648.

Shemiras HaLashon – Lit. "Guarding the Tongue," a book written by
the *Chafetz Chaim* concerning the reward for refraining from
forbidden speech, and the consequences of indulging in it.

Shulchan Aruch – Lit. "The Set Table," corpus of Jewish law written by Rabbi Yosef Karo (d. 1575 CE), divided into four
sections. It is the authoritative compilation of all halachos
governing the life of a Jew in our days.

Simchas Yisrael – a collection of the thoughts of Rabbi Simcha
Bunim of Peshischa (1765–1827), a leading Chassidic Rebbe
in Poland. Published in Petrikov, 1910, by Rabbi Yechezkel
Taube.

Strive for Truth – see *Michtav m'Eliyahu*

Tehillim – Book of Psalms, written by King David with *Ruach HaKodesh* (Divine Spirit).

teshuvah – process of returning to one's commitment to the precepts of the Torah; a written response to a halachic query

Toras Avraham – writings and lectures by Rabbi Avraham Grodzinsky, *mashgiach* of Slabodka Yeshiva

Toras HaAdam – "The Law Regarding Man," a treatise written by the Ramban concerning death, burial and mourning in Jewish law.

Toras Kohanim – "Laws of the Priesthood," book of Halachic *Midrash* on the Book of Vayikra, redacted by Rav (1st generation *Amora*). The original name of the book, given by the Babylonian yeshivos is, *Safra d'Bei Rav*, or just *Safra*.

Vilna Gaon – Lit. "The genius of Vilna," Rabbi Eliyahu ben Shlomo Zalman Kramer (1720–1797), known also simply as HaGra, was the leading rabbinical scholar of Lithuanian Jewry in the 18th century. He is known for his contributions in Talmudic, Halachic and Kabbalistic study.

yetzer hara – the inclination towards evil

yetzer hatov – the inclination towards good

Yevamos – Tractate of the Talmud, chief topic of which is the Levirate marriage

Yoma – Tractate of the Talmud, chief topic of which is laws of Yom Kippur (Day of Atonement)

Yoreh De'ah – Lit. "Give Forth Knowledge," 2nd section of the *Shulchan Aruch*; codifies the Jewish law relating to a wide range of topics, including: food, usury, vows and oaths, honoring parents and scholars, Torah study, charity, circumcision, death, burial, and mourning.

Zohar – *"Book of Splendor,"* multi-volume book of Jewish esoteric wisdom redacted by the 2nd Century Tanna, Rabbi Shimon bar Yochai, based on the lessons in *Kabbalah* he received from his mentor, Rabbi Akiva.

Acknowledgements

This work was made possible because of the cooperation, support, and expertise of many people. It is with much pleasure that I acknowledge Harav Dovid Cohen, shlita, whose gracious enthusiasm, wisdom, and kindness never cease to amaze me.

My appreciation goes to the remarkable Rabbi Ronnie Greenwald who is forever on-call to help a friend, or anyone, in need.

On the editorial side, a big thank you to Rabbi Moshe Armel, whose extraordinary talent and team helped to transform this book into an enjoyable and cogent read. My complete gratitude to Sorelle Weinstein for her unparalleled editing skills; and much thanks to R' Reuven Handler for his keen eye and invaluable insights.

I am indebted to the prolific and talented Rabbi Moshe Goldberger for his on-going and always-sage advice, input, and observations.

I remain continuously grateful to HaKadosh Baruch Hu, Whose infinite kindness and generosity have allowed this book to unfold, and Who has blessed me with my wife, Shira, and my children, who make it all possible and worthwhile.

Please Note

While this book has been vetted to offer information that is sound in *hashkafah*, if you find anything objectionable, please bear in mind that this in no way reflects upon the integrity of those individuals who offered their kind words to this book and who lent their names in support. Editorial changes may have affected content that no longer supports their position or opinion. *The author takes sole responsibility for any errors, omissions, or inconsistencies.* To this end, any comments, suggestions, and corrections are welcome so that this work can be revised for future editions.

About the Author

DOVID LIEBERMAN, Ph.D., is an award-winning author and internationally recognized leader in the fields of human behavior and interpersonal relationships. Techniques based on his nine books, which have been translated into 24 languages and include two New York Times bestsellers, are used by the FBI, The Department of the Navy, Fortune 500 companies, and by governments, corporations, and mental health professionals in more than 25 countries. Dr. Lieberman's work has been featured in publications around the world, and he has appeared as a guest expert on more than 200 programs such as: The Today Show, PBS, The O' Reilly Factor, NPR, and The View.

Infusing Torah wisdom into the psychological process, Dr. Lieberman's talks are enjoyed by people at all levels and backgrounds—*frum* and *kiruv*-oriented alike—and include: parenting, *shalom bayis* (household harmony), relationships, Judaism, self-esteem, singles topics, spirituality, psychology, teens, family, education, and counseling. He writes a bi-weekly column called "Human Nature 101" for The Jewish Press, and is the author of *Real Power* (Feldheim Publishers) now in its third printing, and available at Jewish bookstores everywhere. He lives in Lakewood, New Jersey, with his wife and children.

You can contact the author by email: DavidJay@aol.com or visit www.David613.com for updates and additional information.

ʾREAL POWERʾ

RISE ABOVE YOUR NATURE AND **STOP** FEELING ANGRY, ANXIOUS, OR INSECURE

From the renowned specialist in human behavior, **Dr. Dovid Lieberman,** comes an extraordinary book that shows us how To create a positive and permanent shift in the quality of our lives.

Experience a new kind of freedom and power when you learn how to rise above your nature and move confidently through life without anger, fear, or frustration . . . on ordinary days, and in extraordinary times.

Hard cover ISBN 13: 978-0-9786313-3-8
Soft cover ISBN 13: 978-0-9786313-5-2

PRAISE FOR
ꞌREAL POWERꞋ

"Had Dr. Lieberman lived a hundred years ago he would have been one of the most famous mashgichim in a mussar yeshiva… This is a book, that if read seriously, is going to change your life… it's one of the most important books you're going to read, period."
HaGaon HaRav Dovid Cohen, sh'lita

"If you really desire to turn self-doubt into self-esteem, I urge you to read REAL POWER carefully. This is a terrific book."
Rabbi Abraham J. Twerski, M.D.
Founder and Medical Director Emeritus,
Gateway Rehabilitation Center

"Reading this book is like looking in a mirror. As you turn page after page you realize that this work was written for you and about you. The insights and practical solutions that Dr. Lieberman provides are written with clarity and crispness."
Rabbi Paysach J. Krohn
Internationally acclaimed author and speaker

Haskama by HaGaon Harav Shmuel Kamenetsky, sh'lita

Pick up a copy today at your local Jewish bookstore or online at Amazon.com

·KEYNOTE ADDRESSES·
·LECTURES & WORKSHOPS·

Spanning a spectrum of venues, from Agudah to Chabad and AJOP to Kollel's worldwide, Dr. Lieberman is a highly sought-after speaker, whose engaging and interactive style is enjoyed by people at all levels and backgrounds.

Topics include:
- **Parenting • Shalom Bayis • Relationships • Judiasm • Self-Esteem • Singles Topics • Education • Conflict Resolution • Anger & Stress Management • Teens • Human Nature • Counseling • Kiruv**

INVITE DR. LIEBERMAN TO YOUR COMMUNITY OR ORGANIZATION.

"Dr. Lieberman's blend of Jewish and psychological insights, together with his presentation skills, make him one of the most dynamic speakers that I've ever seen or heard."
Rabbi Yehoshua Kohl
Director of Education and Programming, Gateways

"Dr. Lieberman is our leadoff speaker every semester at our Maimonides program at Rutgers . . . the students love him!"
Rabbi Meir Goldberg, Director, RJX

"Dr. Lieberman brings an audience to life! He's spoken at our branches and by Shabbatons more than two dozen times."
Rabbi Yitz Greenman
Executive Director, Aish HaTorah Discovery

"Dr. Lieberman has 'street credibility' and his bio alone brings people in the doors. He's highly relatable and entertaining, but delivers a potent message the way few can . . . he's probably the best all-around speaker I've ever heard, on any subject."
Rabbi Moshe Katz
Director of Personnel and Training, Torah Links

Email DJLMedia@aol.com Fax 772-619-7828